I thought as a child

as a child

by

Barbara H. Menzies

I thought as a child

First published 1997 by Countyvise Limited, 1 & 3 Grove Road, Rock Ferry, Birkenhead, Wirral, Merseyside L42 3XS in conjunction with the author Barbara Menzies.

British Library Cataloguing in Publication Data.
A catalogue record for this book is available from the British Library.

ISBN   1901231 02 X

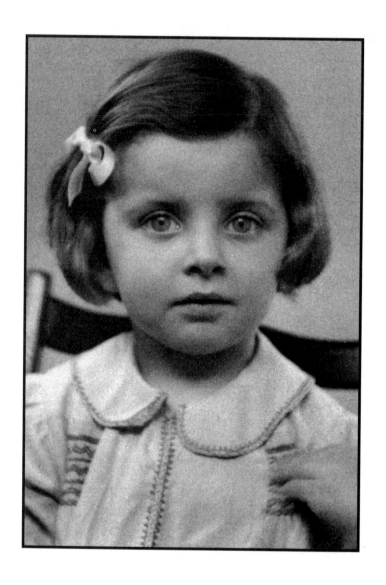

I Thought as a Child

Growing up in St Helens in the 1930's and 1940's

'When I was a child I spake as a child,
I understood as a child,
I thought as a child ..."
1 Cor. 13 v 11

Any attempt to recapture the world of the child by one who has long ago "put away childish things" is at best imprecise, at worst unsound. While seeking to be wholly truthful to personal recollections, these are inevitably coloured by later understanding of past events. It is also acknowledged that others involved in the situations which I seek to illuminate may well interpret them differently. Despite this, I have done my best to describe events in my young life as they appeared to me at the time, as it is the child's world, with all its imperfections, which I seek to recreate.

With this purpose at the forefront of my endeavours I have been sufficiently courageous to refrain from altering the names of people and places, and apologise unreservedly to anyone who thinks I have been too bold in this respect. Wherever possible, exact locations in St Helens are given to enable those who knew the town in the '30's and '40's to identify particular places which they may remember.

I am proud to have spent my early years in St Helens at that time. It was a good place to live. It was a good time to be young.

I am grateful to my Godmother, Marjorie Else, for the interest she has shown in the preparation of this book, and for the time and patience she has devoted to discussing with me both my memories and her own. I also thank my sister, Helen Hathaway, for her helpful comments on the draft copy.

Barbara H. Menzies

1996

I thought as a child

This book is dedicated to the memory of all those talented and highly professional Cowley Girls' School Mistresses who had such a profound effect upon my early education. I thank them all.

I thought as a child

Contents

My first home
22, Hard Lane

It was December 22nd, 1934. Three days before Christmas could not have been the most convenient moment for my Mother to be in hospital giving birth to her second daughter. But such practical considerations did not trouble me, her first-born. Having celebrated my third birthday three weeks previously, I sat in cosy seclusion underneath the living room table.

The deep golden tassels of the chenille tablecloth surrounding my familiar play area added to the feeling of warmth and security. "Baby Darling", my favourite doll, in her long white gown, lay on the carpet beside me, and I happily poured water from the pretty red tin teapot into the doll-sized cups which matched it. That the water was real that day and not pretend was a reflection of the fact that Nana was in charge, and not Mummy.

My doting Grandmother was indulgent, if at times over-protective. On this particular day her mind would, of course, have been preoccupied with her daughter's ordeal at the hospital. Brought up in an age when giving birth was often fraught with danger, and having a tendency to anticipate the worst outcome where illness was concerned, her much discussed "nerves" would undoubtably have been troubling her.

I was aware that this day was special. It would not have been thought appropriate, in 1934, to discuss with a three-year-old the arrival into the world of her baby sister. But all young children are sensitive to atmosphere. Though the words of the adult conversation around me had little impact, the tone of the voices and the non-verbal gestures certainly did. What other reason could there be for my detailed recall of the events of this day?

There was a commotion when my Father came home. I heard the front door bang, and voices were raised in excitement. I sat very still making, at last, some effort to discover what was happening on the other side of the tablecloth. I watched the movement of the familiar adult legs. Nana's long, brown, tailored skirt, made to measure by Mr Breitenstein of Liverpool, left visible a mere three inches or so of thick lisle stocking. I loved her neat, brown size four shoes. Their single strap was fastened each morning with the delicate button-hook with its mother-of-pearl handle. Daddy's highly polished black lace-ups seemed to skip by, as they kicked up the turn-ups on his dark grey wide-legged trousers.

Suddenly, Daddy stretched out an arm, and lifted me out from under the table. He probably told me I had a baby sister. I don't remember that. I remember only two words: 'Let's dance.' Daddy loved dancing. So did I. He twiddled the knobs on the large brown wooden wireless set which stood on a side-table beneath the sash window overlooking the back yard. The wireless had an arched top. The cut-out shapes on its front were shaped like those to be found in stained glass windows, and were covered in dirty brown hessian. After the usual initial crackling and spitting, music burst forth from the hessian covered perforations. We danced. We laughed.

There was not much room to dance in the living room, often known as the "middle" room in this typical middle-of-terrace house. The wall opposite the window housed a large marble-topped sideboard on which was piled the usual clutter of a busy family life. This clutter was doubled in appearance by its reflection in the large mirror which rose from the back of this useful piece of furniture. Opposite the table with its chenille cloth, a fire blazed behind the folding, three-sectioned small brass fireguard, safely tucked away behind the shiny brass curb. There was always a fire in this grate, because it heated the back boiler which supplied the hot water. Originally the old kitchen range with its side ovens had been here, but Nana had initiated some modernisation when her family moved into the house in 1913. The chimney breast was flanked by the usual painted wooden shelves and cupboards. The Singer sewing machine was housed on the shelf at the right-hand side. In front of the fire stood three easy chairs.

We danced as well as we could in the limited space available, then out through the door into the hall. "The hall" was rather a grand name for the space between the front door and the staircase, the hallstand, laden with coats, hats and umbrellas, its drawer stuffed with scarves and gloves, left but a narrow passageway. Undeterred, Daddy led me into the second room to open from the hall, the "front" room.

To go from the middle room to the front room was, for me, to go from day to night, from light to dark, from warmth to cold. A relic, I suppose, of the Victorian parlour, this room housed a display cabinet showing off the finest of our silverware, cut glass and willow pattern china. A dark wooden mantlepiece surrounded the dark blue tiled fire-place. A gate-legged table stood in the bay beneath the sash window, which overlooked the front garden and beyond this, Hard Lane. In the corner stood a four sectioned screen which was probably needed to ward off the draughts from the front door. The room also housed a Welsh dresser, a piano, a gramophone, a record cabinet and a grandmother clock. There must also have been chairs, though I never remember sitting down in this room. As it was Christmas time, the artificial tree, in its red painted tub, clearly marked 10/6 on the bottom, may have been on display. But as Mummy was in hospital, maybe it didn't come out that year. There cannot have been much room here for dancing.

I have no more clear recollections of that day. We may have gone upstairs. Probably it was Daddy who bathed me and put me to bed. It often was. He took off his jacket and hung it on the white painted wooden towel rail. He rolled up his shirt sleeves and knelt on the bath mat. The bath was huge, or so it seemed to an undersized three-year-old who was, as yet, unable to climb in unaided. The taps were wide, but their chunky butterfly tops turned easily in Daddy's large, strong hands. One soaping of Daddy's big hands was sufficient to wash me all over. I stood on the cork-topped stool to be dried on the towel recently warmed over the wooden clothes horse before the fire downstairs. The bathroom floor was covered with black and white checked linoleum. At some point in my early life the side of the bath was "boxed in." A length of shiny black hardboard was placed so as to hide the bath's four ugly duck-like feet and the dark, cobwebby depths beyond them.

A large hand basin filled the space under the window between the bath and the lavatory. The lavatory cistern was way up near the ceiling, and was very noisy. At the end of the long chain which descended from it was a wooden grip which remained out of my reach. At three I don't think I used the lavatory very often. The white enamel chamber pot with its dark blue trim was thought to be more suitable. For some reason now lost in obscurity, this useful object was always known as "the article."

3

Carried downstairs, wrapped in the bath towel, I climbed into my chilprufe sleeping suit, with its convenient "back window." This ingenious contraption, when unfastened, let down the appropriate section of fabric to enable me to sit on "the article" without removing my legs from the bottom half of the suit.

It must have been at about the time that Helen was born that I was promoted from the large wooden cot which stood in the front bedroom to a "proper" bed in the tiny bedroom at the back of the house, beyond the bathroom. Originally this was the maid's room but, by 1934, our maids came only by the day, and went home to sleep. In my small bedroom was a bed, a cupboard and a chair. I don't remember a fire in the small black fireplace, but have fond memories of the little china house which stood on the mantlepiece. It housed an eight-hour nightlight which was replaced every evening. This was a mixed blessing. I was never left in total darkness, but the flickering light did tend to cast ominous shadows around the room.

There were two other bedrooms up the three extra stairs by which the staircase turned onto the landing that ran towards the front of the house. The first bedroom, over the living room, was Nana's. She had a heavy feather-filled overlay on top of the mattress on her four foot wide bed and this was the warmest, cosiest bed I have ever known. Beside her bed was her washstand. Marble-topped, and with a cupboard below, this piece of furniture housed a dispensary of bottles, pill-boxes and ointments, amongst them the two most dreaded tortures of the young child: the syrup of figs and the mustard plasters. On the marble top, Nana's decorative china jug and bowl was surrounded by her many bottles of "nerve tonic" and other essential remedies. On the wall in Nana's room was a large portrait of her Mother, my Great Grandmother, whom I never met. Yet, for me, she was alive in that room. As I moved around, her eyes seemed to follow me. I did not like to be left alone in that bedroom.

The front bedroom was the largest in the house, stretching over the front room downstairs and the hall. Outside its door, on the landing, stood what was always referred to as "the old oak chest." I doubt that it was made from oak. A carpenter from Bishop's Glassworks had made it, and it had served as my Mother's "bottom drawer" before she was married. It stored many treasures. Fifty years later it still housed her bridal veil, the white silk stockings she wore on her wedding day, her confirmation veil, and a lock of her fair baby hair from its first trimming. The bedroom suite had been bought new for my parents' 1930 wedding, and was "modern" for its day. The tall wardrobe had a deep drawer beneath the hanging space, and this served as a linen store. There was a smaller gentleman's wardrobe, with a metal bar inside the door for hanging up ties. There was a chest of drawers as well as a dressing table, and a bedside cabinet, too, with a cupboard for storing the blue ceramic chamber pot.

One of the most fascinating things in this room was the musical box. Nana loved antique shops, and brought this home in 1933, having paid 35/- for it. I have it still. It is French, and plays eight tunes in sequence. Our favourite tune, and one which we played over and over again, was the intermezzo from Cavalleria Rusticana. Whenever I hear this haunting melody I think lovingly of our precious musical box. The spiky metal drum revolves in response to the switch being directed at "joue" and stops when it is turned towards "arrete." A handle is pumped forwards and backwards to wind the mechanism. A glass inner lid protects the workings when the wooden lid, which has a marquetry decoration of holly leaves, is lifted. When I once accidentally backed into the open musical box and sat down heavily, breaking the glass, I am sure everyone was more concerned about the damage to the musical box than they were about the possibility of fragments of glass being embedded in my small bottom.

Looking out of the window of the front bedroom, over the small pocket handkerchief sized lawn, across the road stood "The Abbey Hotel." This was the local hostelry, where Daddy often met with his many friends for a pint of ale. At the back of the house there was no garden, only a flagged yard. Three doors opened into the yard: the kitchen, the washhouse and

22 Hard Lane was a typical middle-of terrace house
opposite the Abbey Hotel.

5

the coal store. Beyond these stood the garage. Ours was the only house in the terrace, I think, to have a garage. The outside lavatory had been demolished to build it. The double doors of the garage opened into the "entry." This alleyway, which ran the full length of the terrace, was so narrow that getting the car into and out of the garage must have been a highly complex operation.

The kitchen of this house was very small. In pride of place stood a cream and green "New World" gas cooker. A row of black enamelled saucepans with pale blue interiors stood on a shelf above it. Beneath the window was a shallow white porcelain sink with brass taps. The wooden draining board leaked drips onto the linoleum covered floor. In the centre of the kitchen stood an enamel-topped table, which had a drawer housing the usual kitchen tools. Standing on my small wooden stool, I would roll my small lump of pastry dough with my miniature rolling pin until it resembled a hard, grey pancake. A wooden meat safe with a metal mesh insert in its door housed all the items which today would be kept in the refrigerator. On top of this the jugs of milk were covered with circles of muslin whose beaded edges prevented them from blowing away. Twice each day Mr Huyton stopped his horse and cart at the gate, and we took our jugs out to be filled from his churn with his pint and gill measures.

On washdays I sometimes took my stool through to the washhouse. On it was placed a small, oval galvanised bowl. I was given warm, soapy water in which to wash my dolls' clothes. You had to stir the water very fiercely to dissolve the soapflakes. For a treat, we sometimes used the soapy water to blow bubbles through my white clay bubble pipe. I was never very good at this. Daddy blew the largest bubbles. Meanwhile Mummy twisted the sheets around in the wash boiler with the wooden "dolly peg," and lifted them with the wooden tongs into the deep sink for rinsing. The final rinsing water would be tinted with the "blue bag." The tablecloths, serviettes, shirts, collars, and even the pillow slips had then to be immersed in a solution of Robin's starch, before the water was finally squeezed out by passing them through the wringer. The wringer was a recent replacement for the old wooden mangle, and had rubber rollers. These, reputedly, were more easily turned than the wooden ones. But I couldn't turn the handle; not even when I gripped it with both hands.

This, then, was my first home. My small, happy, secure world was dominated by the domestic activity within its walls, and which I imitated in my small way with dolls and miniature domestic implements. I lived in this house from my birth to the age of five and a half.

My family
Parents and Grandparents

While others who shared a house with a grandmother might say 'She lived with us,' I have no hesitation in saying 'We lived with her.' The house which I have just described belonged to Nana and, throughout my early years, she was regarded with great respect as the Head of the Family. My Father was happy for her to hold this position. He was a jovial, even-tempered, tolerant person, and tended to concede to anyone's wishes providing they were reasonable.

My maternal Grandmother and her twin sister were born in Birmingham in 1876. The address on their birth certificates, "Back 52½, Suffolk Street" gives an indication of their economic standing and social position. Their father's occupation is given as "Hotel Servant". Nana went to school only from the age of three to the age of eleven, but must have had a good grounding in "the three R's." Her copperplate handwriting, her spelling and arithmetical skills were faultless.

Nana was small in stature, large in "Presence." With her immaculately tailored costumes she wore a clean blouse every day. Some had lace and frills down the front and at the cuffs. Any space at the neckline was concealed with a pretty "modesty vest," which was attached to her blouse with tiny gold safety pins. Each evening her long, wispy locks were braided into a neat plait, and her fringe wound into five metal curlers. Each morning the plait was brushed and wound into a neat bun, secured with numerous hairpins. The curlers were removed, and the five curls were combed into a neat frill, framing her delicate little face. Physically frail and suffering, in her later years, from bouts of severe depression, she showed incredible courage and determination.

Although she came to St Helens shortly after her marriage at the age of twenty two, Nana never lost her Birmingham accent. She was quietly spoken, yet her words always commanded attention. Generous in the extreme, no-one turning to her for help was ever sent away without practical assistance. There must have been many among the workforce at Bishop's Glassworks who had cause to be grateful for her genuine concern and practical help.

Nana was not a regular Church attender, and often seemed to be guided more by superstition and old wives' tales than by religious tenet. Woe betide anyone seen trimming finger nails on a Friday or a Sunday! As a child, my Mother was never allowed to wear green. Nevertheless, Nana had a certain respect for many religious practices. "Churching" she believed, was essential to a mother's recovery from childbirth, and a baby did not "come on" until it had been baptised. Highly suspicious of modern remedies, her medicine cupboard was, nevertheless, well stocked with a wide variety of pills and potions. A fever should be "sweated out," and any sign of a raised temperature was a signal for filling the hot water bottles and piling on the blankets. She was highly suspicious of surgical operations. My Mother claimed that she would not have needed to spend her life breathing largely through her mouth had her Mother consented to her having her adenoids removed as a child.

In 1898 my Grandmother, Rebecca Hathaway, married a widower of forty-two, James Shepherd, whose oldest child, at twenty one, was just a year younger than his young bride. When they came to St Helens from Birmingham, they brought my Grandfather's six youngest children with them. The two older ones were already settled in jobs in Birmingham. The ones still of school age were sent to the Parish Church School, which was then in the building behind the Church, and which later became the Post Office.

My Grandparents took over the management of Bishop's Glassworks and, from 1901, lived at 27, Fraser Street, close to the entrance to the Works. Bishop's specialised in gauge glasses, precision instruments used largely in ships. It was in this house that my Mother was born in 1904. My Grandfather went to register his daughter's birth. That the baby, as the first-born, should take her Mother's name was taken for granted, but he was unsure of the spelling of the extended form of the name he had always used, "Becky". He consulted his Bible, and found the spelling "Rebekah," which is how the daughter of Rebecca Shepherd, formerly Hathaway, came to be registered as "Rebekah Hathaway Shepherd". As she, too, was to be known as "Becky" or, to her Father, "little Beck," the form "Rebekah" was rarely used.

Soon after Mother was born the family moved to 21, Grange Park Road, on the outskirts of St Helens. The house in Fraser Street was retained by Bishops, and became Nana's office. Mother's stepsisters and brothers, each in turn, returned to Birmingham to stay with their older siblings until they had homes of their own. My Grandparents both worked full-time at Bishop's, and my Mother's early upbringing owes more to Katie, who lived in with them and was employed to help in the house, than it does to her parents. Mother loved Katie dearly. Katie took her each day to a small private school in Laurel Road run by two kindly sisters. One taught the children, the other cooked their dinners.

When Katie started courting Joe Graney Mother went along, too. She had happy memories of strolls through Taylor Park, carried aloft on Joe's broad shoulders. But Mother's small life was devastated when business at Bishop's took a downturn, and my Grandmother decided to dispense with Katie's services and stay at home to look after her daughter herself. Katie and Mother wept in one another's arms. They promised to keep in touch. They did, until the day Katie died. After Katie married Joe they lived in

My Mother, 2nd from the left on the middle row, at a small private school in Laurel Road run by two kindly sisters.

9

Borough Road, and Mother visited them often, particularly when there was a new baby to admire. She knitted bonnets for each of Katie's six babies. The first must have taken some effort, as she was only eight years old when Mary, the eldest, was born.

My Grandmother was not a full-time housewife for long. The business must have taken an upward turn quite quickly. Or perhaps Nana did not easily adapt to her new role. Other living-in maids were employed, and Nana continued to work at Bishop's until her death in 1943.

In 1913 the family moved from Grange Park to 22, Hard Lane. Orders for gauge glasses increased during the First World War and, for the first time, women were employed at what we always knew as "The Works." The business must have diversified, too, as a photograph I have of their products at the time clearly shows the manufacture of glass covers for gas mantles. My Grandfather travelled to America to deal with legal matters concerning the export side of the business. The First World War found him stranded on the wrong side of the Atlantic Ocean.

My Grandmother Rebecca,   *My Grandfather Shepherd:*
with her daughter, Rebekah.   *a gentleman.*

My Grandmother, far right, at Bishops' Glassworks

I have only one photograph of my maternal Grandfather. He is standing on the platform at St Helens railway station. On the reverse side of the photograph someone has written "A Gentleman. " He was certainly hailed as a hero for braving the Atlantic crossing at this time. A letter from a "Marine and Railroad Lighting Appliances Electrical Specialities" Company in Arlington, New Jersey, thanks him for his "extreme willingness to hazard the perils of the submarine zone" which, they wrote, was "a cause of admiration." For many months it was considered unsafe for him to make the return journey. I have letters which he wrote home at this time. One is badly stained, has been resealed by the Post Office, and labelled "damaged by sea water."

In the Spring of 1917 my Grandfather was travelling by train across America having, at last, been promised a passage home. The name of the ship and its date and port of departure could not be revealed for security reasons. He promises a cable with the Captain's name, so that his wife could discover where and when to meet him by contacting the American Line shipping office in Liverpool.

At one railroad station, in typical gentlemanly fashion, he was helping a lady down from the train to the platform. He stepped backwards from the train in order to take her hand. His leg slipped between the train and the edge of the platform, badly grazing his shin. By the time he reached his ship, my Grandfather's leg wound had become infected. Each morning he ordered porridge for breakfast, to be served in his cabin, and used it to poultice his leg, By the time he reached home the infection had begun to spread throughout his body. He died in December of that year. My Mother was thirteen years old.

At the age of twelve Mother had started her education at Cowley Girls' School. Unfortunately she did not enjoy her time at Cowley very much, though she made many good friends, some who were to remain friends for life. My Mother lacked confidence, and one or two rather overbearing teachers seem to have caused her to retreat into her shell, and fail to reach her academic potential. But a year at Skerries College in Liverpool, which she enjoyed immensely, soon redressed the balance, and she qualified in 1921 for entry to the F.L. Calder College of Domestic Science.

After an enjoyable two year teacher training course, Mother completed a further year to specialise in needlework and dressmaking. She had always enjoyed, and excelled in all forms of needlework, progressing from making dolls' clothes to making clothes for herself and her friends. Nana bought

Pilkington's Canteen: Miss Kinnings is seated in the centre with Mother on her left.

(left) Mummy and Auntie Marjorie at their Confirmation.
(right) Mother at the F.L. Calder College of Domestic Science in Liverpool.

her a Singer sewing machine for her fifteenth birthday. I doubt whether many similar machines have stitched as many miles of fabric as this one.

Sadly, Mother's confidence again deserted her as soon as she found herself standing before a class of schoolchildren. Jobs were not easy to find in 1924, and her first teaching post was at a school in Nottingham. She enjoyed her new surroundings, and got on well with her kindly landlady in Sherwood Rise. But the children at the school gave her a hard time, and she was worried about her Mother, who was ill. She came home to St Helens before completing her first year's teaching.

My Grandmother's responsibilities at Bishop's appear to have been much greater after she was widowed. A telephone was installed at home so that she could be contacted whenever there was trouble at the Works. At any hour of the day or the night she was prepared to go back to Parr to speak to the men. Although she arrived home from these excursions in a highly agitated and exhausted state, it seems that she was invariably successful in resolving the workers' disputes.

Nana must have been pleased when her daughter returned from Nottingham. Mother's next post, at an Evening School in Newton-le-Willows, allowed her to live at home. She enjoyed this work. The Students were older and better motivated. By this time there was a temporary lodger living at 22, Hard Lane. Doing one of her many good turns, Nana had offered accommodation to a Miss Kinnings, who was working as Supervisor at Pilkington's Cowley Hill Plate Glass Works Canteen. The Kinnings' Family were also involved in the manufacture of glass tubes. Miss Kinnings soon persuaded Mother to join her in the pursuit of "good works" and she found herself joining the "Band of Hope." She also found herself registered as a collector for donations to "St. Agnes' Home" which was at the time described as "a home for fallen women"! Soon she joined Miss Kinnings as Assistant Supervisor in the canteen and, when Miss Kinnings retired, she took over as Supervisor. This was the post which she held until her marriage in 1930.

The young of the 1920s had a lively social life. In line with current fashion, Nana had finally allowed her daughter to have her hair "bobbed", and to make herself a knee length frock with no sleeves, the waistline somewhere around the hips. Mother and her young friends organised a series of "subscription" dances, charging 1/3 entry fee, which included the home-made refreshments. Mother recalls the time when she and a friend carried between them a large wicker clothes basket filled with sandwiches, sausage rolls and cakes all the way from Hard Lane to their latest venue in Boundary Road. On more than one occasion, Nana had to be approached for a subsidy when expenditure exceeded income, due to lower numbers attending than had been expected. After the garage was built in the back yard, this was cleaned out and decorated on several occasions, and the gramophone set up ready for a dance. There were fewer financial headaches when the organisers did not have to pay for the hire of a hall.

Mother and Father in Mother's open-topped tourer.

My Father enters the picture at about this time. As he seems to have had a reputation for shyly hugging the walls, puffing continually on a cigarette he was not, at first, encouraged to attend the subscription dances. But inevitably, due to a shortage of male partners, Mother and her friends were obliged to include him.

There were not many private cars on the roads of St Helens in the 1920's. Nana bought an open-topped tourer for Mother in 1923. Mr Cook, who sold it, took her out in it a couple of times to show her how to drive it, and to point out the "nipples" which she would need to keep greased. The same Mr Cook sold bicycles to Helen and me twenty years later. DJI841 clocked up many thousands of miles, and gave a great deal of pleasure to a large number of people. This was the age of driving for pleasure and "going for a run" in the car was a rare treat. Saturday afternoon trips to Southport became routine, and holidays were spent touring the South of England. In Summer evenings Mother could often be seen driving round St Helens with Katie's three little boys sitting in a row on the back seat.

Driving was a great adventure in those early cars. There are several hairy stories of occasions when the brakes failed. Mother would not have risked parking anywhere but on level ground, with the wheels turned inwards towards the kerb. One day, driving up Windleshaw Road, she was amazed to watch one of her wheels glide across the road into a field on the right hand side.

After they started "going out" together, Mother taught Father to drive, and his Mother and Sister were included in the Saturday afternoon trips to Southport. Father joined Mother and Nana on their touring holidays. After visiting relatives in Birmingham they continued to the South coast, the journey taking several days. They certainly reached Lands End. I have a photograph to prove it. Porlock Hill in Devon was one of the greatest challenges for DJ1841. Even in bottom gear, the engine rebelled. Undeterred, Father turned the car round, and it climbed the hill, slowly and painfully, in reverse gear. The hill successfully negotiated, the passengers got out to admire the view while, with bonnet raised, the radiator puffed out clouds of steam and eventually cooled sufficiently for the journey to continue. After their marriage, Father seems to have taken over completely the responsibility for driving the family cars, although Mother continued to renew her driving licence. Neither of them, of course, ever took a driving test.

Father was born in the same year as Mother, 1904. As a young child he seems to have lived under a rather repressive regime, although the photograph of him swinging on the gate at his birthplace, 83, Windleshaw Road, would indicate that he was a lively toddler. His Father was a dour Scot, reserved, gentle and softly spoken, and was probably kind but strict with his two children. The main problem I had with Grandpa Menzies was one of communication. His quiet Scottish burr was often difficult to interpret when he spoke without removing his pipe from his mouth. I frequently misunderstood what he said.

My paternal Grandfather came to St Helens as a youth from the Scottish countryside near Blair Atholl, where his Father was gamekeeper on the Aukleeks estate. As gamekeeper he befriended the Pilkington family from St Helens, who called upon his expertise during their "hunting, shooting and fishing" holidays in the area. The Pilkingtons were impressed with Donald Menzies' youngest son, John. I think he must have been a bright lad. One of his wedding presents was a copy of Dean Farrar's "Life of Christ," inscribed "from John's first teacher, Glenochty School." He was twenty six when he married, but she had not forgotten him. As there was little work to be had in Perthshire at the time, John was invited to join Pilkington's glassworks as a clerk. He accepted, and remained a loyal Pilkington's worker until his retirement.

The culture shock for this Scottish youth on coming to St Helens must have been severe. But it was eased by his kindly landlady, Mrs Penketh of Harris Street. In 1896 he married her lovely auburn-haired daughter, Ellen Jane. My paternal Grandmother was undoubtably the dominant personality in that marriage.

Adults and children alike tended to mind their p's and q's in Grandma Menzies' presence. The rules by which she governed her own life and the lives of those around her lacked the flexibility to which the Shepherd

My father as a child, with his Mother, Father
and sister in the Pass of Killiecrankie.

family was accustomed. Mother always felt uncomfortable when invited to the Menzies' home, 55, Kiln Lane, for tea. One did not stray from the narrow path of seemly behaviour if Grandma happened to be looking. As my Father was so obviously at ease with his Mother-in-law, it was unfortunate that my Mother was so ill at ease with hers.

On her own admission, my paternal Grandmother found it difficult to forgive those who sinned. Yet, to all outward appearances, she lived the life of a devout Christian. On Sunday my Father was not even allowed to ride his tricycle and his sister, seven and a half years older, was confined to "uplifting" reading. The family attended Church twice on Sundays and, after they built a bungalow, "Weem" in Chapel Lane at Eccleston, had their own pew in Christ Church.

Both Father and his sister Eva were well trained in punctuality and tidiness. Father always folded his clothes with military precision when he took them off, and the creases in his trousers were well pressed, as he carefully laid them beneath his mattress each night. I suppose it was early training, too, which led him to disappear into the lavatory precisely at seven o'clock each morning, and to emerge promptly at seven fifteen. Eva's tidiness was carried to even greater extremes. When pushing Father up Windleshaw Road in his pram she would be seen tucking his hands neatly beneath the coverlet. If he wriggled them out again he received a sharp slap on the back of his hands. A family friend certainly has cause to recall Eva's obsession with tidiness. One day, as she rose from her chair to illustrate some story she was telling, Eva jumped up and straightened the chair. Poor Mrs Baxter, a rather large, portly lady, sat down heavily on the floor.

Eva was a victim of "bronchiectasis" and was always described as delicate. Each morning she hung over the edge of the bed and coughed, to clear her lungs. She was very tall, very thin and very pale. She was never allowed to take a job or to marry, though she would have liked to have done both. On falling in love with a young St Helens barber, who was anxious to marry her despite her infirmity, she must have been devastated when her Mother forbade it. Eva and Bert Roberts were both artistic and enjoyed going out sketching together. However, Eva's health would have made bearing children dangerous. And there was another seemingly insurmountable obstacle to her marriage. Bert was a Roman Catholic.

So Eva stayed at home and painted. She also played the violin. A youthful Eva once took her violin along to a Church social at St Andrews. And nobody asked her to play. The compilers of the programme for the evening were left in no doubt as to the gravity of their sin of omission. They were suitably repentant, and apologised. But my unforgiving Grandmother vowed never to set foot in St Andrews Church ever again. And she never did.

After a short time at Miss Jackson's school in Dentons Green Lane, my Father continued his education at Cowley Boys' School, which was then alongside the Girls' School in Cowley Hill Lane. This building was later to be taken over by the girls and christened "South Block." Then, at the age of fifteen, my Father went as a boarder to Rossall School at Fleetwood. There were initially, I believe, a few clashes between his Mother and the school authorities. The biggest disagreement, much to my Father's embarrassment, concerned the wearing of underpants. I can only assume that his Scottish ancestry and the issue of what is, or more accurately what is not worn under the kilt led to his being forbidden to wear these garments. The school objected but, due to Grandma Menzies' immovable stance on the subject, was forced to concede. To my knowledge, my Father never did wear underpants.

My Father entered into boarding school life wholeheartedly. I think he enjoyed at Rossall a freedom he was not allowed at home. He played rugby and joined the O.T.C. His tuck box, which I still have, was well stocked with tins of baked beans and condensed milk. These came in useful to restore his energy after cross country runs along the breezy shore behind the school. His St Helens accent disappeared almost completely, and he learned to smoke.

After leaving Rossall at the age of nineteen Father joined his Father in an office at Pilkington's Glassworks. By the time of his marriage in 1930 he was based at Pilkington's London office. Mother and Father's first home was a first floor flat at 22, Cranley Gardens in Muswell Hill. They soon settled to their new life and were very happy. Mother enjoyed housekeeping, and walked her landlady's dog down to the station each evening to meet Father on his way back from work. Nana furnished one room in the flat for herself and planned to visit them often. She enjoyed London, too. Unfortunately, their tenancy of the Cranley Gardens flat was to be short. The depression of 1930 made the outlook for Pilkington's London branch uncertain. The offer from my Mother's cousin Sidney, for my Father to join him in a rapidly expanding radio wholesale business in Liverpool was tempting.

Cowley Schools: South Block on the left, North Block on the Right.

On this postcard which he sent home in 1919,
Father has marked his seat in the Dining Hall.

Father at Pilkington's Glassworks, far right.
His Father is standing next to him.

My Parents came home to St Helens in October, 1930, after only four months in London, and moved in with Nana at 22, Hard Lane. I was born in December, 1931.

My Father excelled as a travelling salesman, and soon became popular with the owners of the many small radio and electrical businesses in the area. Never at a loss for words, he enjoyed a good chat. In 1932 Uncle Sidney initiated him into the Amity Lodge 3904 in Liverpool, and he became a loyal Freemason. The golden Jubilee magazine published by the Lodge recalls my Father as "that colourful personality and excellent speaker!" As young children we all enjoyed playing with the small globe-shaped pendant which hung from his waistcoat by a gold watch chain. It opened out into what I thought resembled a tiny gold man but which was, I believe, some kind of Masonic symbol.

Although my Mother, too, had many friends, she did not join any organised groups and her interests remained largely domestic. She dedicated her whole life to caring for her house and her family. Three cooked meals were dished up every day. At mid-day Nana's meal would be served into small white basins, covered with saucers, and packed into a shopping basket. A young office girl would arrive to carry the meal down to Bishop's on the trolley bus, where it would be re-heated. The high standards which my Mother always maintained in cooking, dressmaking and laundering were legendary.

A proud Mother with baby Barbara outside the Abbey Hotel.

My baby sister

Helen

The front door bell rang for the third time that afternoon. Mummy knew what the caller would have to say and sent Elsie, the maid, to answer the ring. It was the same message we heard so often: 'The baby's crying.' A concerned middle-aged lady would be standing on the doorstep clutching a bunch of flowers. They always carried flowers, these ladies who thought we weren't taking proper care of our baby. They were on their way up to the Cemetery to tend the graves of their loved ones. Was that why they sounded so self-righteous? Maybe they were justified in implying that we were negligent in not attending to the loud wails coming from Helen's pram, which stood on the front lawn.

And why was no-one paying attention to the crying baby? Because Helen spent most of her waking hours crying. Rocking the pram, and making the usual reassuring "cooing" noises had no effect whatsoever. What does puzzle me, in retrospect, is why we didn't put the pram in the back yard when Helen was taking her obligatory daily allowance of fresh air. The problem was only solved when a sympathetic Dr Merrick assured us that to feed our hungry baby more frequently than at the prescribed four-hourly intervals would not do her any lasting damage. He also suggested that no-one would blame Mummy if she supplemented her breast milk with the occasional bottle of Ostermilk.

Poor Mummy wasn't used to a hungry baby. I had had to be shaken awake every four hours at that age, and then it had been difficult to persuade me to take the required amount of nourishment. Despite the regulation

23

two weeks in bed following Helen's birth, Mummy took a long time to recover her strength. And this despite being sent by her Mother for Churching the moment she left hospital. Nana also urged her to hasten the Baptism as a possible cure for Helen's constant crying, so she had to plan and organise a Christening party while being hardly fit to do so. Helen and I were both Christened when we were only three weeks old.

Eventually the baby thrived and the crying lessened. As a precaution we never went anywhere without a good supply of spare dummies, in addition to the one in Helen's mouth. And often there was a bottle of milk, wrapped in a muslin nappy, hidden away in the bottom of the pram. But in those days there was no clever device for preventing the milk from leaking through the rubber teat, and that nappy would be decidedly milky by the time we got home. The crescent-shaped bottles had a teat at one end and a valve at the other. The rubber valves sometimes used to spring across the room when they were being stretched across the hole at the end of the bottle. I used to chase them and bring them back.

I held tightly to the pram handle as we walked down Greenfield Road to do the shopping. Marfords, on the corner of Hard Lane and Greenfield

My baby sister: Helen

Road, supplied the groceries. Sometimes we left them a list and they would deliver our order later. But sometimes we waited while they weighed out our sugar and flour into tough blue paper bags, and sliced our bacon on the slicing machine. The lids of the 7 pound biscuit tins were made of glass, so you could peer in and choose your favourite variety. We walked down to Johnson's to get the bread. If Mummy wanted to stop at the Post Office on the way I would wait outside with the pram. Miss Dilloway, the Postmistress, was a very frightening lady, and I don't think she liked children. Sometimes she was even cross with grown-ups.

There was a great deal of interest in our baby, for she was a handsome child, who liked to be propped up on the pillow so that she could look around. A small fair curl was developing on her previously bald head, and this was being carefully nurtured into a "cupee" with the soft bristled baby hair brush. Now where the word "cupee" came from, or whether I have spelled it correctly, I do not know, Perhaps it was something to do with Cupid? Helen and I both had "cupee" dolls. They were made from celluloid, and were short and fat with moulded fair curls on their over-large heads. They resembled the children drawn by Mabel Lucie Atwell.

I dreaded the inevitable question from passers-by who paused to peer into the pram. I knew what they were going to ask me: 'Can I have her?' Even at three years old I knew this to be an extremely silly question. Grown-ups surely knew that you did not offer them your baby sister, as you might offer them one of your sweets? They knew what the answer had to be, so why did they ask the question? But I was forced to play their silly game and say 'No.' On other occasions, to deny a grown-up what they asked would undoubtably have been considered rude. The rules of etiquette were very confusing.

It was also cause for embarrassment when friends and relatives lifted me up for a hug or a kiss. We were not an overtly demonstrative family. The only time I remember my Mother kissing me was when I was coming round from the anaesthetic after having my appendix removed at the age of nineteen. Yet Mummy and I were very close. I was never left in any doubt that I was loved and cherished. We were all loved. And loved equally. It is to the credit of each of the three adults closest to me that I never felt the slightest twinge of jealousy towards either my sister or my brother.

Helen and I were as different as the proverbial "chalk and cheese". We earned our respective places in the affections of the rest of the family in quite different ways. That I was labelled "good" as a young child probably owes more to laziness than to any advanced sense of moral rightness. I quickly learned that it was much easier to conform. I disliked raised voices, arguments, anything that disturbed the domestic peace. I still do. If I thought I was treated unfairly I tended not to protest, but to swallow my resentment until bedtime, when I could release my hot, angry tears in private, beneath the bedclothes. Helen was quite different. She, I think, quite enjoyed a battle, and did not mind the noise which I hated. Often she was the cause of it!

When she was very small, we soothed Helen's anger with a dummy dipped in honey. And when she couldn't sleep a teaspoonful of brandy sometimes helped. Helen's cot was sometimes in the front bedroom and sometimes in Nana's room. I think they must have taken turns. Often I would be sent upstairs to search for missing dummies. These slimy objects, when new, had air in them, but were quite quickly sucked flat. By the time I had retrieved them from underneath the cot and the bed they were covered in fluff. I gingerly picked them up by their bone rings, avoiding the messy rubber part. Each evening half a dozen of these essentials to a peaceful night would be scalded, placed between two saucers, and deposited in a handy position by the bedside.

In every family there are dates of note. One such date for us was November 23rd, 1936. One month before her second birthday, and having reached the stage when she was "into everything," Helen had followed Elsie upstairs. A loud howl sent everyone running into the hall. A hurt and extremely angry toddler lay on the cold tiles. After unsuccessful attempts to pacify the injured baby, Dr Merrick was summoned. He was unable to detect any broken bones, diagnosed bruising, and left. But the yelling continued, and Helen would make no attempt to walk on her injured leg. Eventually, after several visits by the doctor, an X-ray was suggested. This was arranged for December 8th, more than two weeks after the accident, and revealed a greenstick fracture. The leg was belatedly encased in plaster of paris. The crying ceased, and Helen quickly found a suitable mode of travel on her bottom, dragging the plastered leg along beside her.

Helen has always claimed that Elsie pushed her down the stairs. I find it difficult to believe that our loyal and faithful maid could possibly have been responsible for harming our precious baby. My memory of Elsie is of a tall, pink-clad friend! Our maids wore frocks of heavy cotton in a dusky pink colour. Unlike the maids at the houses of most of my friends, they didn't change into a black frock for the afternoons. But they did change their aprons. All the aprons were white, but those worn in the morning were overall-type garments with long tape fastenings which threaded through eyelets. In the afternoon these were exchanged for smaller aprons which were only waist high. When we had a new maid, Mummy would be busy on the sewing machine shortening, lengthening, taking in, letting out or whatever alteration was needed to make the uniform fit. After our maids ceased to wear uniform the pink dresses and the white aprons were used for dressing up when, later, we made up our plays and concerts.

Helen's leg was in plaster when we went to a Christmas party, and she attracted a great deal of attention because of it. The party was in a large hall, and the Mothers who were staying sat on a row of chairs along one side. Helen sat on the floor at Mummy's feet. She was passed all sorts of party goodies to keep her entertained: balloons, crackers and the like. I wonder if this was the start of her obsession for collecting all the bits and pieces of party trappings at every party we went to? She would often sit clutching the fancy wrappings from parcels, crackers and cakes, and we were not allowed to go home without them. She guarded her treasures avidly, and was always reluctant to leave them in order to join in the games.

I was more interested in the games. I loved party games, particularly singing games. "Here we come gathering nuts in May" was my favourite. Winning and losing was of little concern. I preferred ring games like "Here we go round the mulberry bush" where no-one was ever "out" and we could all go on singing and dancing right to the very end.

Saturday afternoon excursions to Southport had become routine before Helen and I were born, and we were taken along from a very early age. Both Nana and Daddy arrived home from work in time for our mid-day dinner on Saturdays. After dinner we strapped Helen's pram to the luggage rack at the back of the car with the brown leather straps, and set off for Southport. We parked in the narrow road behind Bobby's (later Marshall and Snelgrove, and then Debenham's) and went into the store by the back door. After looking round Bobby's we walked down Lord Street to look at the other shops. In the Summer Daddy sometimes took me to the beach while the others did the shopping. But we always met back at Bobby's for tea. We took the pram up in the lift because the café was on the first floor. From the café you could see right down into the ground floor through a large circular hole in the floor. This had a rail round it, and a large tree grew up from the ground floor almost to the ceiling of the first floor. At Christmas time the tree was decorated with hundreds of fairy lights. The tables all had white linen tablecloths, and the waitresses wore white caps and aprons over their black frocks. Our special waitress lived in Rainford. We always sat at one of her tables. In an alcove an orchestra played gentle background music. Plants in pots divided the orchestra from the customers.

Our waitress was always pleased to see us. She was particularly pleased to see Helen because she was fond of babies. If the Staff weren't too busy our waitress pushed Helen's pram into the kitchen so that everyone could see her. And she took Helen's bottle to heat it up. Sometimes one of the Staff would give Helen her bottle while we had our tea. The tea came in a silver teapot, with a silver hot water jug, milk jug and sugar basin to match. We had sandwiches and cakes and little packets of chocolate finger biscuits wrapped in silver paper and bound with strips of bright blue paper. I loved these, but was only allowed to have one if I ate all my sandwiches first. Then I could eat half the packet of chocolate finger biscuits, Nana re-wrapped the other half, and put it in her bag to take home. Sometimes she let me eat these in the car on the way home.

One of these trips to Southport was particularly memorable. Helen had progressed from the big pram to the folding push-chair, and it was this which was strapped to the luggage rack that day. When we arrived in Southport we discovered that the waterproof apron from the push-chair was missing. It must have fallen off during the journey. Everyone was upset. It was very worrying. It was unlikely that it could be replaced. Teatime at Bobby's that day was not very happy. On the way home we stopped at every shop we passed, in Ormskirk and in Rainford, to enquire whether the missing item had been handed in. It hadn't. I was very upset, and Helen's pram cover featured prominently in my dreams for some time following this incident. As I was also a sleepwalker, I expect this caused me to take one of my night-time walks.

The Greenfield School of Dance

My whole body tingled with excitement as we neared the bottom of Greenfield Road. As we opened the small metal gate and looked up at the open door of the large building, through which the strains of the music from "Coppelia" could be heard, I could hardly breathe. I was blissfully happy. This was my favourite place. A whole week was far too long to wait for the next dancing lesson. And now it was Tuesday again.

I had "soft blocks" for ballet, being too young, at four, to do any work on "points". I also had red tap shoes with shiny metal plates on the soles, and wide ribbon laces. I had two home-made tutus, one white, one pink. Often we sat to watch the older girls. Then it was my turn. The barre which ran down the long side of the room, with the mirror behind, was too high for me. I wished I could reach it. Those of us who were too short for the barre stood in a row in front of it. We practised the five positions. Then there was the opportunity to skip round the room in time with the strong beat on the piano. This was the part I enjoyed the most.

At the end of each session we formed a line. Each in turn would progress across the room showing off some clever acrobatic leap. Some could do three cartwheels in a row. When it came to my turn I was content to turn and run to the back of the line again. I longed for the day when I would be able to perform these amazing tricks, too.

(left) I had two homemade tutus, one white and one pink.
(right) Dressed for Aladdin at the Pilkington Theatre.

We were practising for a competition which was to be held in Liverpool. My music was Dvorak's Humouresque, and I can remember the steps to this day. Mummy made me a beautiful, ankle length striped taffeta frock with puff sleeves, and I had a tiny black hat with a feather in it, secured by an elastic thread under my chin. I also had a woolly black toy cat to hold. The fact that I was supposed to be depicting the rhyme "Ding, dong bell, pussy's in the well" was explained to me years later. At the time I had no idea that this was the intended aim of my dance. Auntie Vie, Mummy's cousin, came to stay. She liked to play the piano. She obtained a copy of my "Humouresque" music, and played it for me to practise at home. But she played it far too slowly, much more slowly than Miss Johnson's pianist. I knew it was wrong. But she persuaded me to adjust my timing to hers.

The competition was a disaster. When my turn came I climbed the steps to the huge stage and looked down into the vast audience. It was very awe inspiring. By the time I had recovered my composure and remembered what I was supposed to do, the pianist had already started to play my tune. Valiantly I went through the well-practised routine. But the pianist finished long before I did. I continued to the end, then dropped my very best curtsey.

The audience clapped. Mummy met me as I climbed down the steps from the stage. I could tell by her face that I had not done very well. I was sorry.

This disappointment did nothing to lessen my enthusiasm for the dancing class, and the following Summer I had an opportunity to redeem my reputation. All Miss Johnson's pupils were taken up to Rainford Hall at Crank to dance on the lawn at a Garden Party. This time Miss Johnson's pianist played the piano for my dance, and all went well.

I never lost the initial thrill, as we entered the building at the bottom of Greenfield Road each Tuesday. And we had such fun preparing for the pantomimes which Miss Johnson produced at the Pilkington Theatre. "Aladdin" was my favourite. Mummy made two Chinese outfits for this. One had yellow trousers edged in black. The black tunic top was edged in yellow, and had a yellow dragon on the front, The small, round black cap had a yellow turned-up brim and a yellow tassel. The other outfit was made from shiny white satin, edged with orange. The top was covered with brightly coloured flowers. Its matching cone-shaped hat had a imitation plait which hung down the back.

Because the show would finish late I went to bed for a sleep in the afternoon. Mummy came into my bedroom to wake me up. She was carrying the brown wooden tray with the metal handles, and it was covered with an embroidered traycloth. There was a boiled egg in my chicken eggcup, and the thin bread and butter was on my fairy plate. The fairy danced round the rim and, printed in orange letters beneath the bread and butter were the words "Dinky dances with the bee, to the tune of a buzz and a fa-la-dee. " I sat up. There could not have been anyone in the whole wide world as fortunate as me. Here was my favourite tea, lovingly laid out with great care, and soon I was to dance on the stage in the theatre in my Chinese costumes. My feet prickled beneath the bedclothes, and I can recall the sensation as clearly as if it had happened yesterday.

Mummy sat by my bed while I ate my tea, then we got ready to go to the theatre as soon as Daddy and Nana got home from work. The Chinese costumes and my black dancing pumps were packed in the small black suitcase with the soft, shiny top and the red and white lining, and the tall conical hat with its pigtail stood on the top. No doubt our current maid would be staying late that night to babysit with Helen.

The Pilkington Theatre, in the 1930's, was on the Prescot Road site, alongside what I think we called "Ravenhead Works", and where the Head Office stands today. We parked the car and hurried into the theatre. It was very dark, and seemed to me to be very late. This added to the excitement.

31

There was a great hubbub in the dressing room, and many of the adult helpers were already looking rather harrassed. I was handed over, and Mummy, Daddy and Nana went to take their places in the audience. I can vouch for the fact that the thrill traditionally associated with "the smell of the greasepaint" is no myth. I can recall the smell of the stage make-up to this day. My face and lips duly coloured, I was helped into my yellow and black costume.

The routine of the first two choruses completed, we sat in a row on a long, hard bench to wait for our next turn. It was a long wait and we had to be very quiet. Then a very large, very flustered lady appeared, and shouted 'Who's in the finale?' I had never heard that strange word before, so I assumed the "finale" didn't concern me. But I began to feel uneasy when some of those around me were putting on their white outfits and their pointed hats. As they were handed their coloured paper lanterns on their long wooden sticks I realised that this must be the last scene, and I should be there, too. The others left. I sat alone. Then someone noticed me and said 'Aren't you in this?' 'Yes' I wept miserably. 'Why didn't you say so?' demanded the large, cross lady who had announced the finale. I was too upset to reply.

I was hustled into my white costume, and a lantern was thrust into my hand. I was pushed onto the stage, and joined in as the others were partway through the routine. All too quickly, the pantomime was over. My make-up must have been smudged by a few tears. But the cold cream used to remove it helped to ease the tension.

I continued to attend Miss Johnson's dancing class in Greenfield Road until the start of the war in 1939. Then, disaster, Miss Johnson closed down her School of Dance. I was devastated. I begged to be taken up to Prescot Road to Miss Peet's Dancing Academy, which some of my friends attended. It was too far. It couldn't be managed. There was another small baby to be considered by then, and Daddy, who had been in the Territorial Army ever since leaving school, was expecting his "call up" papers at any time. At seven and a half I was sure I could find the way alone, a trolley bus into town, then change onto the tram for Prescot. No, I was told. In the Winter, with the blackout, that was not feasible. I cried a lot. The sheets on my bed must have been very damp and salty. Especially on Tuesdays.

This experience left a raw wound which took years to heal. And there were times when the wound re-opened and hurt again. When the ballet music from "Coppelia" was played on the wireless, or "Humouresque" I felt compelled to listen, despite the pain. And, some years later, I was taken to the cinema to see "The Red Shoes." I wasn't the only one who cried all the way through, because it was a sad story. But I wasn't crying only for the dancing heroine, I was also crying for myself.

Showing off my "Ding dong bell" dancing costume in the garden at Cranley.

Starting School:
September 1936

The two main entrances to Cowley Girls' School were reached from wide and imposing steps, rather like those to be found before a Town Hall or a Palace. I felt like a Queen, I was four and three quarters, and it was time to start school. As we climbed those steps I nearly burst with self-importance. We pulled the push-chair up backwards, and Helen held on tight. We entered the huge building, and turned left into the main corridor. The room at the end was the Office, and we went there first. We paid the fees and we got the receipt. I think it was two guineas. Then we went into the cloakroom. The black metal clothes pegs were very high, and could only be reached by standing on the wooden benches which covered the wire mesh shoe lockers. My coat and hat were hung on a peg, and my outdoor shoes were changed for rubber soled slippers with elasticated tops. I felt very grownup.

The Form Room was the first on the right, beyond the entrance doors, Mummy introduced me to Miss Fitch, then she and Helen left. I was sorry for Helen, because she was too young to stay. Miss Fitch welcomed me kindly, and thrust a small wooden spade into my hand. Indicating a metal tray full of sand at the front of the room, she pointed to a small girl already digging, and said 'This is Sarah.' Sarah Wiswall was my first school friend. She and I played together. She came to my house, and sometimes I went to tea at Garswood Gates Farm, where she lived. Sarah and I dutifully turned the sand over with our spades on our first morning in school. I don't remember the sand tray after that first morning. I wonder where it disappeared to?

Miss Fitch was our teacher for the first two years. The first year we were called "Kindergarten". The second year we were called "Transition". Miss Fitch's chair and table stood on a wooden pedestal at the front of the room. I don't know why it was thought necessary for Miss Fitch to be elevated above the floor, for she was a very tall lady, and we four and five year olds were all quite small. Miss Fitch was very thin, and she was very pale; rather like Auntie Eva. I think she must have been delicate, too. She had a cough. On her desk was a tin of glucose and a teaspoon. From time to time she replenished her energy from the tin.

We sat at small wooden desks in rows facing the pedestal, behind which was the blackboard. The windows on the left of the desks were high, and were opened and closed by means of a hook at the end of a long pole. The Caretaker used this pole on dark days, when he came in to light the gas mantles. He pulled down the metal rings to release the gas, then there was a "pop" as his lighted wax taper came into contact with the gas. I was glad when the afternoon was sufficiently dark to warrant lighting the gas mantles. They gave a warm, cosy glow, and made a friendly flickering background sound as we coloured in our purple outlines of Ruth and Rover.

Cowley Girls' School

The thick wax crayons were not very suitable for keeping within the lines, but we did our best. I could have made a better job with the pencil crayons which I had at home.

Along the back wall of the room ran the shelf which housed the "toys". My favourite was a box of wooden picture cubes. There were nine cubes, and you could make six different pictures. You turned the cubes till you found the picture you wanted, then arranged them in lines. I also enjoyed the peg boards with the coloured wooden pegs. You could make an endless variety of interesting patterns with these. The box of tiny orange rubber building bricks was quite good, too, but there weren't enough bricks to build a proper house. All these things could keep you busy for quite a long time. Unlike Hansel and Gretel. Hansel and Gretel were wooden dolls. By the time you had removed their clothes, then replaced them, you had exhausted their entertainment value. I was not impressed with Hansel and Gretel.

At one end of the shelf was a pile of black paint boxes and a tray of glass jars for water. When these were given out you hoped you would get a box where the colours could still be recognised as being different from one another. In some, each block of colour had deteriorated into a dirty shade of grey. We painted within the lines already drawn for us on the small duplicated sheets of paper. The lines were always the familiar purple ones, reflecting the usual colour of the duplicating jelly. If you used too much water the colour strayed beyond the lines. If you used too little, you couldn't lift any of the colour from the box onto the brush. Our efforts stood along the tops of the radiators to dry. They curled up in the heat and had disappeared altogether by the next morning.

At the other end of the shelf was a pile of wooden boards and, beneath the shelf at this end, a galvanised bucket. Inside the bucket, wrapped in damp hessian, were twenty or so balls of grey clay. I dreaded the days when the clay boards were distributed. I did not appreciate the clay. It posed too many problems. It felt nice, and was good to squeeze. But the directions for its use were disheartening. Always one was expected to produce an animal. And four long sausages, which were all I could manage to represent legs, would never support the heavy lump of clay which was the body. With clay I was a total failure, and suffered acute embarrassment as Miss Fitch walked up and down the aisles between the desks to inspect the models.

Weaving was not a great success, either. The coloured wool was very attractive, but it was difficult to weave it through the strings on the cardboard without pulling these out of shape. I never completed a whole card either to my own or Miss Fitch's satisfaction. I would be unravelling my work to try again while the others had their's off the cardboard, and were sewing them into little purses.

A trip across the corridor into the hall was always a treat to be enjoyed. There were three reasons for going into the hall: one was Prayers, one was Singing Games and one was Anne Driver (I think that was her name). For Prayers we stood in two semi-circles, Kindergarten at the front and Transition behind. Sometimes it was Miss Fitch's turn to say prayers, and sometimes it was Miss Pearson's turn. We had only two words to remember: "Our Men." But we did sing. I was glad when it was:

> Good morning, Mr Sun, happy morning, Mr Sun,
> All the little birds are singing, every one,
> For they can't sing in the night,
> When there isn't any light,
> So they have to wait for Mr Sun,
> To make it warm and bright.

I have remembered this song because it made sense. I have always had difficulty in remembering things which don't make any sense. Some of the songs we sang at prayer time didn't make any sense, like 'pity mice in plicity.' 'All things bright and beautiful' was nice. I liked the tune. Another good tune, but with puzzling words, was 'Crown him, crown him, all the little children'. And sometimes we sang a very sad song with a sad tune: 'Little birds in Wintertime, hungry are and poor.' Anyone with a birthday stood at the front, and we sang a special song for them. Then we gave five enormous claps (or six, or seven) while Miss Fitch or Miss Pearson pulled their hair (not very hard) five, or six, or seven times.

Singing Games were my favourite activity. Sometimes Miss Pearson's Form came, too, and we made an enormous circle, almost filling the hall. My favourite was "Oats and beans and barley grow," but I liked "In and out the dusky bluebells" too. Sometimes we played the same games as we played at parties, like "Lucie Locket lost her pocket." We never played enough of these games for my liking, and I was always sad when it was time to stop.

I liked Anne Driver, too, though she wasn't a real person. She was a voice in a little brown box mounted high on the wall in the corner of the hall. It was odd that a voice without a body was saying 'Good morning, children'. Did she have eyes? Could she see us? I think she could, because sometimes she said 'That was a good skip, (or hop, or jump).' Often she wanted you to crouch down and then jump up, but she had some good music which helped you to know when you should be down and when you should be up. It was fun. When she said 'Goodbye', we said 'Goodbye,' too. Could she hear us?

Occasionally we marched down the cinder track to the "patch." Later there were to be air raid shelters here and, later still, tennis courts. But in 1936 it was a rough, grassy area with a long, thin flower bed along the edge. Here we played "What time is it, Mr Wolf?" This game was a bit dangerous. You had to turn and run away so suddenly when someone shouted 'dinner time!' that there was a good chance of bumping into someone else and falling down on the rough ground. But consolation was to be found in the Cookery Kitchen which was down in the basement. Here there was always someone who dispensed bandages and chocolate as you sat on the wooden bench beside a homely array of cooking utensils.

Of all the things which we did in Kindergarten and Transition, I think I enjoyed reading the most. The bookcase was on the wall opposite to the windows, near the door. The introductory book was green, and had only a few words. There was Ruth and Rover and Kitty. There was a boy, too, but because I have forgotten his name it is clear that he didn't make much impression on me. On the front of each book was the title "Beacon Readers" with the picture of a flaming torch. It was such a challenge to progress to a new book. I always had my eye on the next colour: blue, orange, red. Most of these books simply had words to remember. Words to read, of course, were not as interesting as stories to read. Story books were scarce, but there were some flimsy paperbacks of very few pages printed in black and white. These stories were a delight. There was a story about the North Wind, and one about the Gingerbread Boy. When you had progressed to book four of Beacon your reading book was thicker, and you could read about Careful Hans, and forget about Ruth and Rover. You had had enough of them. By this time I was reading "What Katy did," "What Katy did at school" and "What Katy did next" at home. Mummy had read these books when she was a little girl.

Halfway through the morning was milk time. School milk cost one halfpenny, and chocolate biscuits cost one penny. You lined up beside Miss Fitch's pedestal to hand in your money. Mine was in a little leather purse which hung from a leather strap round my shoulder. Sometimes I had enough for two biscuits. They were delicious, covered in thick chocolate. Miss Fitch warned me to eat only one, and to take the other home. The milk came in small bottles with cardboard tops. When you depressed the centre of the cardboard circle it dropped down, leaving a neat hole into which you could insert the straw. At least, that was the theory. It didn't always work. If the bottle was too full you and your desk would be showered with milk. It was embarrassing to have to go to the cloakroom to fetch the smelly cloth to clean up the mess.

The smells from my childhood seem to have persisted in my memory equally as vividly as the sights and the sounds. The cloth, the clay, the paints, the wax crayons, the chocolate biscuits all had their distinctive smells. So did the lavatories. There were regular times for visiting them. It was a long walk, and we went in a line. Down the stairs, through a store full of games equipment, and across the playground. Then we passed the coal heap. It was forbidden to stand on the coal heap. One naughty boy had once done this, we were told, and had disappeared down the hole into the cellar below. Miss Fitch stood well away from the lavatories, directing the traffic from the back. I didn't blame her. The flushing system was very poor, as was the state of the wooden seats. In fact, you were lucky to find any kind of seat at all covering the cold porcelain. In Winter, of course, the whole system was frozen, yet we were still expected to use the dreadful place. I wonder whose job it was to deal with those lavatories afterwards? In case of emergency, or in a torrential downpour, we were sometimes allowed, as a treat, to use the lavatories in Miss Pearson's room. There were two here, one for girls and one for boys, clean, and always in good order. Miss Pearson's Form could use them all the time.

I don't ever remember being deliberately naughty in school. Contrary to popular belief, I think that very few children are. I was always anxious to please. Most children are. I thrived on praise. Most children do. And if I made a mistake it was because I hadn't understood what I was supposed to do. And that was because I was a very poor listener. If you have faulty hearing, I think you tire of the effort to hear, and lose concentration. You don't realise that you have missed something, and make the best sense you can of what you have heard. And sometimes you get the wrong message. If you are not sure whether you have the right question, you are reluctant to offer an answer. I was conscious of switching my attention away, at times, from what was going on in the Form room. I was becoming a dreamer.

Miss Fitch was like me in one respect. She didn't like too much noise. I wanted to please her. So I was very quiet. But then she worried because she thought I was too quiet. Some grown-ups are very difficult to please. Miss Fitch and Mummy talked in the cloakroom. Mummy was surprised. I had plenty to say at home. Why didn't I talk at school? Miss Fitch had an idea about how to persuade me to talk more. She would invite me to tea.

So one day Mummy took me all the way down to the other end of Hard Lane, the City Road end. Miss Fitch's house looked a bit like ours from the outside, but it was quite different inside. The first thing she showed me was the bathroom, which was on the right just inside the front door. This was a great surprise. I had never been in a house where the bathroom was downstairs. Then another surprise: we went upstairs to the living room. Miss Fitch had made a big effort for her young guest. She had brought Hansel and Gretel home for me to play with while she got the tea ready. I wished she had brought the puzzle cubes. She made sandwiches and cakes and jelly. Her kitchen was upstairs, too. I don't know whether I was more talkative after this visit, but I was always quite fond of Miss Fitch.

Three weeks at the start of the Summer Term in 1937 were spent at a different school. Nana was to be admitted to the Royal Infirmary in Liverpool for some tests, and a rest. Her duodenal ulcer was troublesome at the time. We were going to stay with Mummy's cousin, Uncle Sidney and his family at "Aldridge," Druids Cross Gardens, as this could be convenient for hospital visiting. Daddy worked with Uncle Sidney in the warehouse at Edge Lane, so it would be handy for him, too. During this time I was to go with Uncle Sidney's son, Stanford, who is three months younger than me, to Beechenhurst School on the corner of Druids Cross Gardens and Menlove Avenue. The contrast with Cowley couldn't have been greater.

Beechenhurst wasn't like a school at all. It was simply a large house. Inside it was bright and cheerful, painted in warm pastel shades, with white interior doors. The doors, in particular, impressed me. I don't think I had seen white doors before. The doors at Cowley and at home were dark brown. Until then I hadn't realised how much dark green and dark brown there was at Cowley School. I resolved that when I had a house of my own it would have white doors. We went into what seemed to me like the front room of a house, with a large bay window. Here were about eight or ten individual small tables and chairs, painted in pink and pale blue, and arranged in a circle. There was also a toddler's tall chair with a wooden tray attached. I suppose the child who sat here was about two years old. The rest of us were four or five.

I think the teacher decided not to overtax my brain, as I was only a temporary pupil. Either that or she mistook my age: I was very small. She gave me a lace and a box of wooden beads to thread on it.

Later we did some counting with the abacus, and copied some numbers onto little individual blackboards. I was glad when Mummy told her that I knew how to read, because then she found some books for me, and I was very happy. We had milk at Beechenhurst School, and took our own biscuits with us. The milk wasn't in bottles, it was served in little mugs with pictures on them. The girl in the tall chair had orange juice instead. She wore a bib.

After school Mummy and Auntie Freda came to meet us, and brought Helen in the push chair. We went for a walk in Calderstones Park before going back to the house for tea. There were lots of daffodils in the park, and it was very sunny. Stanford lived in a large house, and there were stables at the back for Uncle Sidney's horses. While we were staying in Druids Cross Gardens we could visit Uncle Ernie and Auntie Clara, because they lived in the same road. Their house was called "St Moritz." Their front door impressed me. It had a circular insert of pretty leaded lights. Uncle Ernie was Uncle Sidney's older brother. He had two sons, Maurice and Bobby. Maurice was a handsome youth of fourteen. He wore long trousers with his school blazer, and I admired him greatly. Bobby was seven, but I was wary of him because he played very rough games.

We went to visit Nana at the hospital. The walls inside the hospital were a bit like those at Cowley, because the lower half was covered with shiny dark green tiles. Nana was in a little room by herself. While we were there a nurse brought her some ice cream in a little glass dish with a funny flat spoon, and she shared it with me. The X ray of Nana's duodenal ulcer had been examined, and she had been told that she had a deformed duodenal cap. This seemed to cause her a great deal of worry. Her weight at the time was recorded as 7st. 6lb. Dr Wallace Jones had prescribed a special diet, and would send his bill for 3 guineas for the consultation. The Royal Infirmary charged 6 guineas a week.

On Saturday morning we didn't go to school, so Stanford and I went with Uncle Sidney and Daddy to the warehouse in Edge Lane. There was a huge room where we could play, and we spent most of the morning playing hide and seek amongst the many large cardboard cartons which were neatly stacked in rows.

Uncle Sidney and Auntie Freda were very kind, and so was the teacher at Beechenhurst School, but I was glad to get back to Cowley. There we did "proper" sums on squared paper, and "proper" writing on paper with double blue lines to help with getting the letters the right size. Also, we wanted to get back to St Helens to see how our new house was progressing.

41

Moving house

Helen had to hold on very tightly to the sides of her push chair, as we pushed it along the dark, rough, gritty surface of Eaton Road. We veered to left and right, avoiding the large puddles. It was fun. We had pushed Helen up Hard Lane, and had turned left opposite Cowley Boys' School, because we were going to "the house" to talk to Mr McCall. It was February, 1937.

Beneath the sign which said "Eaton Road" was another which said "Unadopted." But we had been told that someone would adopt it soon, and make it into a real road with a smooth surface and footpaths. Someone did. Twenty five years later. One year after we had moved out of "Cranley", our Eaton Road house. It was called Cranley because our parents' London flat had been in Cranley Gardens.

Cranley was hardly recognisable as a house in the early Spring of 1937. It was more like a pile of bricks in the middle of a large field. Mr McCall was in charge of making sure that it turned into a proper house. There was a rule that you couldn't build a house in Eaton Road costing less than £1,000. That was a lot of money. But Nana would live with us, so we could use some of her money, too. A sitting room downstairs and a bedroom and a dressing room upstairs would be hers. The final cost of this five bedroomed house with its extensive grounds was about £1,600.

On the right hand side of Eaton Road other houses were being built, their gardens stretching back to the railings and the trees which formed the boundary of the cemetery. But Momma and Dadda Toddy's house had been there for a long time. It was called "Windyridge," and it was one of my favourite places to visit. I had known Mr and Mrs Stoddart all my life, as they were the parents of Mother's best friend, and I suppose my early attempts to pronounce their names had resulted in these rather odd pet names. "Momma and Dadda Toddy" they remained, and were addressed by me as such for the rest of their lives.

On the left hand side of Eaton Road a vast area of waste ground stretched down till you reached the back of the Rainford Road houses. On one side this space was bounded by the entry behind the Hard Lane houses, and on the other side the gardens of the houses on the left hand side of Kingsley Road. Our house would face the garden of the house at the top of the right hand side of Kingsley Road, where the Scott family lived.

Summer approached, and the puddles in Eaton Road dried up. But you still had to take a snake-like path along the road, in order to avoid the pot-holes. We took deck chairs with us, we took a picnic, and we took our buckets and spades. The workmen had dug a large square pit, and the carpenter from Bishops had lined it with wood. It was filled with sand. Sand was always freely available at Bishops, being an essential ingredient in the glass-making process. And there were always handymen from "The Works" willing to do odd jobs for us. I expect they were glad to supplement their meagre wages. And my Father certainly never showed any interest in D.I.Y. Mother blamed this on the Menzies' family's obsession with

We played in the sandpit while the house was being built.

43

tidiness. Father would never have been allowed to make a mess, so wasn't able to practise any potential handyman's skills. Personally, I doubt whether practice would have had any effect. I take after my Father in this respect. I was certainly never restricted in this way but, like him, find it difficult even to knock a nail in straight.

One weekend the carpenter was back erecting a swing and a seesaw. Lots of friends came to play with us in the garden that Summer. We watched the builders at work. And hindered them too, I expect. One builder in particular must have found it difficult to get on with his work when I was around. He was my favourite. He was my first love, and I wish I could remember his name. We talked at length. He treated me like a grown-up, and I forgot that I was only five and a half. I wondered if he would like to marry me? Unfortunately, he told me, that wasn't allowed until I was a bit older. So I promised to try to grow up quickly, and he promised to wait for me.

We were lucky to have a very large garden at Cranley. There was a second plot of land behind the house, on a lower level but, as it would not have easy access to the road, it could not be used for building and we acquired this land as well. So our garden was only separated from the playing fields of the Open Air School (now the Hamblett School) by the narrow entry which gave access to a side gate into the cemetery.

Daddy in the Cranley garden, during the building of the house.

*Cousins Audrey, Valerie, Brian and Juliet Hathaway with other friends
enjoying the swing and the see-saw in the Cranley garden.*

The garden was landscaped as the house was being built. 850 yards of
turf were purchased, at 10d a square yard, and 250 golden privet trees, at
30/- per 100 were planted around the boundary, together with 125 ordinary
privets at 20/- per 100 and 125 thorn bushes at 12/- per 100.

The day the green wooden Summer House was delivered was very
exciting. The builders had laid a circular concrete base and now - here
was the Summer House! It was Nana's Summer House; a present from
Bishops for the new house. The metal device at the centre of the base was
to enable the Summer House to be rotated. The theory was, I suppose,
that it could be gently turned towards the direction of the sun at different
times of day. But this took no account of the imagination of the many
young children who were to play in this garden over the following years.
We children gave one another rides on this new and exciting roundabout,
whizzing it round at great speed. It provided us with endless entertainment
as a house, a shop, a hospital, a ship, a train, and even a cafe. At last,
many years later, it ground to a halt, its mechanism rusted, and could no
longer be moved to face the direction of the sun.

I failed miserably in my attempt to visualise the finished house and
garden. I had thought the front gate would face Eaton Road, and when I
was told it was to face Scott's house, I suffered considerable unease. Could

they have failed to realise that if you put your gate in front of a house, you wouldn't be able to get out? Had I been brave enough to express my worries, I could have been told that the width of the road would separate the gate from the fence of the house next door, and I would have been spared weeks of unnecessary anxiety.

I have no recollection of a moving day, but it was in October that Heaton's removal van transported all our belongings from 22, Hard Lane to 16, Eaton Road. It took them nine hours and they charged 10/6 an hour. As with many similar properties, 22, Hard Lane wasn't sold, it was rented. We visited our old home each week to collect the rent, write the amount in the small brown book, and listen to the catalogue of repairs which awaited our attention. I am sure that Nana would have kept the property in good repair, and doubt whether she would make much profit from the small rent which she received.

Meanwhile, we were all settling in at Cranley. Nana had a longer walk to the trolley bus at "the top of the Green," and we had a longer walk to school. "The top of the Green" was an interesting place. It was here that the trolley buses turned round. When they arrived at the top of Dentons Green Lane the conductor would bring out his long pole, and transfer the

Barbara and Helen with cousins Beryl and Roy
Hathaway outside the Summer House.

two trolleys from the "up" track to the "down" track, ready for the bus to go back into town. The fare to the Lingholme was ½d, and you could go all the way to the Sefton Arms for 1d. The tickets were clipped on the conductor's machine which was suspended from his shoulder. There was a bell to signal to the driver: two rings for "go" and one ring for "stop." A large notice at the front of each bus declared that spitting was not allowed, by order. At the other side of the Green, on the Kiln Lane/Rainford Road corner, stood a very old cottage. And outside the old cottage there often stood a very old lady. She was bent and wrinkled, and we children thought she might have been a witch. She was dressed in black, and her frock reached down to her ankles. Sometimes in the Summer time she sat on the pavement outside her cottage in an old upright chair. She was probably lonely. Perhaps she would have liked us to stop and chat. But we never did. We hurried past as quickly as we could.

There were no pavements in Eaton Road because it was unmade. Each time the fireplaces were cleared of ash, this was carried out in a galvanised bucket to fill in the potholes outside the gate. My knees were bandaged more frequently than before: the black grit of Eaton Road tended to lodge painfully beneath the skin of grazed legs.

There were two doors at Cranley. The front door was large and impressive, and opened into a porch which sported a black metal umbrella stand. This door was, however, rarely opened. It was usually locked, and sometimes it was difficult to find the key. Only strangers came to the front door. And Dr Merrick. If Dr Merrick was coming the key would be found, and the door would be standing open ready to receive him. If it was an unexpected stranger, we would lean through the window of Nana's sitting room, and redirect them to the side door. The side door was rarely locked, even when we were all out. And if it was locked, everyone knew where to find a key. There was always a spare one hanging on a nail inside the outside lavatory, which stood alongside the side door. The outside lavatory was a good place to hide if we were playing out of doors. The top half of the door was louvred and, if we stood on tiptoe, we could peep out.

The side door opened straight into the scullery. This had a tiled floor, and a pantry opened from it. The pantry had wooden shelves for plates and dishes, and small hooks along the front of the shelves supported cups and jugs. In the corner under the small frosted window stood the meat safe. On top of this was the enamel bread bin and the milk jugs with their muslin covers. The scullery window overlooked the back garden on the cemetery side, and beneath this was the conventional white porcelain sink with its wooden draining board. There was an enamel topped kitchen cabinet which had a cupboard and three drawers.

In an alcove alongside the pantry stood our New World gas cooker, and above it a wooden cupboard to house the pans and baking tins. This was not a good idea, as it was quite dangerous to stretch up to get something from this cupboard if there were already pans and kettles boiling on the cooker. We discovered just how dangerous this was the day the fat in the chip pan caught fire. The cupboard above the cooker was totally destroyed.

There was no wash house at Cranley. Each week the dirty sheets, towels, tablecloths and shirts were packed into a brown paper parcel, listed in the buff coloured notebook, and left ready for collection by the man from the Providence Hospital laundry. Each week he returned our parcel of clean laundry, which we checked and ticked off in the book. I enjoyed counting the pillow slips, and laying out Daddy's starched collars in a neat row. The other clothes were washed in the kitchen sink, and the handkerchiefs were boiled in a huge pan on the cooker.

In 1939 we acquired our first washing machine. This was supplied by the St Helens Corporation Gas Department. Mummy had chosen the de-luxe model, and was unable to afford the purchase price of £6 11s 3d. So she opted for the 13/6 deposit with 12 quarterly payments of 10/6. This machine was nothing like the present day automatic washing machine. First you filled it with five gallons of cold water. Then you added the soap. Then you operated the "agitator," a sort of metal version of the old wooden dolly peg. Then you lit the gas beneath the washer, to heat the water. This needed a long spill, because you couldn't get near enough with a match. Having immersed the clothes, you then repeated the agitation process. This was quite hard work. You then passed the clothes through the rubber wringer, and drained the dirty water from the machine by means of a tap. You needed a bucket for this. The process was repeated with rinsing water, each five gallons being heated before the clothes were immersed. Even then you weren't finished, because the scum then had to be scoured from the inside of the washer with hot soapy water. The scullery floor would be as wet on wash days as the floor in the old wash house at 22, Hard Lane. And Mummy still needed her rubber galoshes.

Another addition to the scullery at about the same time was a huge gas refrigerator. Nana was a bit suspicious of the fridge. She insisted that milk taken from it should 'have the chill taken off it' before it was safe for us children to drink. And we still used the old meat safe for the meat and any left-over cooked foodstuffs. For some strange reason the fridge had a curved top surface, making it difficult to rest anything on top. This was a pity, as there weren't many surfaces on which to put things down in our scullery. The washing machine, however, was designed to convert to an enamel table top, as the wringer folded down inside the drum when it wasn't in use.

A door from the scullery led to the kitchen. This was warm and cosy. Here was the modern version of the old fashioned kitchen range. It was called the "Yorkist" and was finished in smart apple green. Beside the fire, which had an adjustable canopy and damper, was an oven which had an ingenious pedal operated opening device. This was very handy if you needed to open the door and were clutching the roasting tin containing the sizzling Sunday joint in both hands. Above the fire and oven were hot plates, concealed behind double tile-fronted doors. I don't think the hot plates were used for cooking very much, as the gas cooker was much quicker. Sometimes the vegetables were transferred to these plates for simmering. However, this recess was often used to air clothes, and also to dry the "sticks" for lighting fires. This sounds like another dangerous practice. I don't think anyone was very safety conscious in the 1930's. A back boiler heated the water, and this whole magnificent contraption was priced at £27 15s.

Beside the "Yorkist" range stood the coal bucket, and behind this the tall black flue brush. Cleaning the flues was a very sooty job, which needed tackling every Friday. On the ceiling before the kitchen fire was the wooden clothes rack which was lowered and lifted by means of a pulley, the rope being wound round a double metal hook fixed to the wall. When we removed the warm, dry clothes we would blow the smuts from them. On a windy day the fire often blew a puff of dust and smoke into the room.

At the left hand side of the kitchen range were wooden cupboards, painted green. They stored a miscellany of items from tinned and packet foods to cleaning materials and shoe brushes. I enjoyed tidying them when they got in a muddle, which they did frequently. My tidying up was not always appreciated. I liked to arrange the packets, tins, bags and boxes in neat rows in order of size. It was a long time before I understood that this was not the most useful way to organise a deep cupboard where some things were needed daily and some only once a month. Perhaps it was feared that I had inherited some of Auntie Eva's fettishes!

Above the door from the kitchen into the hall was a glass fronted box with a double row of small metal plates which jolted from side to side when bell pushes in particular rooms were pressed. They were labelled lounge: nursery: sitting room: dining room: bedroom 1: bedroom 2: bedroom 3: bedroom 4: bathroom. Bedroom 5 didn't have a bell because it was only a boxroom, though it was big enough for a bed and when we had a maid who lived in, she slept there. The bell in the bathroom hung down above the bath, on a cord from the ceiling. Although we continued to enjoy the services of a maid after we moved to Cranley, I don't ever remember her being summoned by a bell.

Before the fire in the kitchen stood the table with the chenille cloth, and on the wall which backed onto the Nursery was the marble-topped sideboard. Its mirrored back had been discarded. Most of the people who came to our side door were invited to sit on the chair which stood beneath the kitchen window and have a cup of tea before they left. I have clear memories of the man from the "Prudential" sitting here, as did the man from the Providence laundry, Mr Huyton the milkman, Mr Fogget from Marfords who delivered the groceries, and the "Stop me and buy one" ice cream man, who left his tricycle parked by the front gate.

The hall at Cranley was huge, and had a polished wood block floor. All around the hall, at about 20 inches from the ceiling was a dark brown wooden shelf, displaying a collection of about a dozen decorated plates. Each Spring these would be brought down to be washed, and the plate shelf relieved of its accumulated dust. And there was some dust in that house! Cranley was heated solely by coal fires, apart from a small, ineffective electric convector heater in the hall. We had very large fires in the lounge, and the one in the kitchen only went out on Fridays, in preparation for cleaning the flues.

Each Spring Mr Cooper would arrive with his large bag of brushes to sweep all the chimneys, and each room would be swathed in dust sheets. We would be sent outside to report the appearance of the stiff black brush as it emerged from each chimney pot. After Mr Cooper's departure, the whole house would be ready for its very necessary thorough Spring cleaning.

The hall table and the Grandmother clock had pride of place in the hall. There was no longer any need of the hallstand, for Cranley had a cloakroom. The coat pegs along one side were high, for grown-up coats, and those along the other side were low, for children's coats. At the bottom of the cloakroom the new cream telephone stood on a wooden shelf and round the corner was a wash basin. Then there was "under the stairs." This was a dark, dusty, musty area which stored old pieces of carpet, together with various brooms and the Ewbank carpet sweeper. I always hoped I wouldn't be asked to fetch anything from under the stairs, as this was a favourite haunt of spiders and other insects.

At the front of the house, next to the porch, was Nana's sitting room. This was a lovely room, and caught all the morning sunshine. The furniture in this room came from the front room at Hard Lane. Here Nana had her gate-legged table, her display cabinet, her piano and her screen. The original intention had been that she would sit in her own room in the evenings in solitary seclusion. Of course this never happened. We had been used to living together as a family, and continued to do so.

There were two other reception rooms, the lounge and the nursery, which would later become a dining room. During the time in which the dining room was a nursery, the large dining table stood in the bay in the lounge, which overlooked the garden. We sat on the window seat with its covered dunlopillo cushion, and tried not to drum our heels on its painted wooden sides. This was not easy at a stage when our feet would not reach the floor. If the cushion was removed from this seat, lids could be lifted to reveal storage space underneath. It always smelt a bit musty in these storage boxes, and anything left in here for any length of time was inclined to accumulate a layer of mildew.

The fireplace was down at the bottom end of this long room, and we sat close to it in the Wintertime. No matter how high the fire was built up it was always cold at the other end of the room.

Double glass doors opened from both the lounge and the nursery into the loggia. This draughty area had a tiled floor, and, wide open spaces where you would normally expect windows and doors. If the weather was good enough to sit in the loggia it was good enough to sit in the garden, as the loggia didn't get a great deal of sun. Perhaps an open-sided loggia wasn't such a good idea after all.

But the nursery was an excellent idea. Lots of space for lots of toys! Helen and I were both doll lovers, and were beginning to accumulate a large supply of dolls' furniture, prams, clothes and teasets. There were puzzles, games, story books, colouring books and crayons. We were very lucky children. With a vast number of friends and relations, we were showered with birthday and Christmas gifts, and sometimes gifts in between. We spent many happy hours in that room, and so did our friends. And it got in a terrible mess. Sometimes you could hardly open the door because of the clutter behind it. And it was often a very noisy room, too. There were the usual arguments when we both wanted the same thing at the same time, and I think I must have been unbearably bossy when I was trying to organise a game of "house" or "school." We had the old "wind up" gramophone in the nursery, and our own set of records. There were several collections of Nursery Rhymes, and our favourite tune: "The teddy bears' picnic". In the corner of the lounge stood a brand new modern radiogram. We were very lucky to have this, but as Daddy was a representative for the Hathaway radio wholesale business, he was easily able to purchase such items.

The Cranley staircase was impressive. The lowest stairs were shaped, curving outwards to form a wider step at the bottom. On the half landing, the ledge below the coloured stained glass window housed an intricately carved wooden galleon with brown parchment sails. Here the staircase turned, and the final few stairs led onto a large, open, airy landing. Here stood the old oak chest, now covered in a beige and blue cloth cover with a pleated frill, and edged with dark blue binding. This provided a handy resting place for the early morning tea tray.

Nana's bedroom was on the right, above her sitting room. Her Mother's portrait hung above her pale yellow wash basin. Her marble topped washstand was now in her dressing room and, among the usual array of bottles and pill boxes we put, each evening, a tray of cups and saucers with a jug of milk, a basin of sugar and a teapot. Nana had an electric kettle - it must have been one of the first - and she was in charge of the early morning tea. She brought it round to us in her dressing gown, her plait hanging over her shoulder and her metal curlers resting on her forehead. On Saturday mornings there was an additional ritual. Helen and I were presented with a small thin glass of clear liquid to be drunk before we had our tea. This was not an unpleasant drink. It consisted of a teaspoonful of sugar dissolved in hot water, to which had been added a couple of teaspoonsful of fluid magnesia.

My parents' room was on the left at the top of the stairs, above the lounge. Here they had their furniture from the front bedroom at Hard Lane, but a much nicer view from the bedroom window. Beyond the large garden and the playing fields of the Open Air School was Rainford Road and Windle Island, the traffic island where Rainford Road crossed the new East Lancashire Road. As in Nana's bedroom, there was an attractive tiled fireplace in this room, too, and a wash basin.

The bedroom next door where Helen and I slept had the same view. Nana had bought a bed for Helen to match mine, and we had discarded the cot. We had a wash basin, too. I always associate this bedroom with A.A. Milne's stories and rhymes. Mummy sat on a chair by my bed, and read a whole story or some of the rhymes each night. Helen usually fell asleep partway through, but I lapped up every word, practically living in that forest with Pooh Bear and his friends. I wept for poor unfortunate Eeyore, sympathised with silly old Tigger, and loved little Piglet best of all. And, of course, I was full of admiration for Christopher Robin. If anything, the rhymes affected me more than the stories. Why, I wonder, did I so often insist upon hearing about the Dormouse being forced to give up his geraniums red and delphiniums blue, and live among yellow chrysanthemums instead? It was so unfair. What had the little dormouse done to deserve such treatment? The doctor should have known better. I cried my heart out for the poor innocent little creature. I was also extremely sorry for poor King John. To have to send Christmas cards to himself to cover up the fact that no-one loved him enough to send him any seemed to me to warrant sympathy no matter how many bad deeds he may have committed.

When we had guests to stay, which was often, they slept in the cold, dark bedroom next to ours, which overlooked the cemetery. You couldn't actually see the gravestones, because of the large trees. This room had dark furniture, and didn't get any sun.

The fifth bedroom was tiny. It didn't even have a wardrobe. It just had a curtain across one corner, hiding about four or five wall hooks. And as it didn't have a fireplace it had to have a small ventilation grill in the wall. Most of the time it was full of boxes, left over rolls of wallpaper, and anything else that didn't have a home elsewhere. This room overlooked the drive and the garage, and separated the bathroom from the lavatory.

The lavatory had a little room all to itself. The cistern was low down and had a lever instead of a chain, and the seat was not made of wood, it was made of pearl green cellulite. There were cream tiles on the walls, with a green line separating the top row from the rest. There was mottled green lino on the floor, and a shaped green rubber mat to put your feet on.

The bathroom was big, and the bath was six feet long. There was plenty of room for Helen and me to get in together. It had a shelf for the soap, and a huge mirror on the wall behind it. Its front and end panels were made from shiny green vitrolite. All down the wall opposite the bath was a fitted cupboard which contained the hot water cylinder and slatted shelves for storing linen and airing clothes. Outside the bathroom stood an oak corner washstand on which stood Nana's old jug and bowl. These were for decoration purposes only, now that Nana had a wash basin in her bedroom.

You could lock all the bedroom doors at Cranley, as well as the bathroom and lavatory ones. They each had a keyhole and a key. And the downstairs rooms locked, too, with an ingenious device which I suppose was intended to fool the burglars. On the hall side of each door was a circular knob, which turned away from the door catch to lock it, and towards it to unlock it. For a short time after we moved in, these downstairs doors were locked every night. But we quickly gave up this nightly chore.

One morning we were all having breakfast around Nana's gatelegged table in the sunshine in her sitting room. Eggs and bacon were the usual breakfast fare in those days. I was eating a piece of fried bread with an egg on it. Helen had finished hers, and had disappeared into the hall. I don't think she should have left the table, but she was being naughty, and refused to come back. Then she had a novel idea. She locked us all in, and either couldn't or wouldn't unlock the door again. Perhaps she couldn't. It was a bit tricky. After a fruitless conversation with her through the locked door, the casement window was opened, and I was lifted through. Fortunately the side door was unlocked, and I was able to get through to unlock the sitting room door so that the rest of the family could escape.

Daddy and me looking out of the open-sided loggia.

Measles, Chicken Pox and Terrible Earache

I was in bed again. It happened frequently in 1938. If I was ill I was always in bed. Sometimes being in bed wasn't too bad. In the daytime I transferred to Mummy's and Daddy's bed where there was plenty of room. The rash was either dabbed with calamine lotion or dusted with Robin's starch. It itched, but scratching wasn't allowed. I could hear the children from the Open Air School when they came out to play on the field. That made me think about what my friends were doing at Cowley: were they playing out, too?

Measles wasn't too bad. Chicken pox itched more. Even a paste made from bicarbonate of soda and cold water didn't ease it for long. The sheets on the bed must have been very messy. If I got out of bed after dinner and looked through the window I could see the three-sided shelter on the Open Air School field. The canvas camp beds were laid out in rows, and the children were covered with blankets. The teacher sat on a chair at the front of the shelter, reading a book. It was very quiet. Then the teacher stood up and blew a whistle, the children got up, and made a great noise as they ran out onto the field to play.

Getting better was never boring. It was the best part, really. There were always plenty of comics and books, and there were colouring books and crayons. I remember "Chicks Own" and "Tiny Tots." Their very titles are an indication of their content: children were encouraged to prolong their innocent childhood much longer in the 1930's than they are today. "Rainbow" was another favourite: a substantial comic with games and puzzles as well as stories and comic strips. Sometimes there were books full of cardboard dolls to cut out, and clothes with tabs round the edges to attach them to the dolls. You had to be careful not to cut off the tabs. And you had to be careful not to cut the sheets. When Nana came home she always came upstairs with a new comic, or book, or game, or some new crayons. Sometimes, when Daddy came home, he would come upstairs and play "squares." He drew rows of dots on paper and we took it in turns to join them with either a horizontal or a vertical line. If you completed the fourth side of a square you wrote your initial in the square, and had another turn. Then we counted to see who had won the most squares.

I nearly always had to stay at home for three weeks, in order to avoid passing on the infection at school. When I went back to school after having something infectious my desk would be empty. I had to start again with new books. We always knew when Miss Fitch had a note to say that someone had measles or mumps or chicken pox or scarlet fever. She sent for the Caretaker, who put that person's desk outside the door. Later it would be removed, and it would come back a few days later, empty, and having been "stoved" and its contents burned. These desks had a funny smell for weeks afterwards.

Dr Merrick visited regularly whenever anyone was ill in bed. For something very minor, like a cough, we would go down to his surgery in Bickerstaffe Street. Surgery hours were 9-10 in the morning, 2-3 in the afternoon and 6-7.30 in the evening. On Sundays and Bank Holidays there was a morning surgery only, and no surgery on Wednesday evening. How, I wonder, did Dr Merrick find time to visit all his patients at home, daily when necessary, and attend all home confinements, too?

The door into the waiting room of the surgery opened straight from the street. It was very dark: the walls were brown, and so was the linoleum on the floor. An assortment of very old and very uncomfortable upright chairs lined the walls, which were badly in need of a fresh coat of paint. Once your eyes were accustomed to the gloom you would notice the solemn faces of those who had arrived before you. It was important to scrutinise these faces well. When they had all disappeared, and the only ones left were the ones who had arrived after you, then you would know that it was your turn. No-one ever spoke. If you had something that you really must

56

say, then you had to whisper it very quietly in Mummy's ear. There were two doors opening from the waiting room, one for Dr Sugden and one for Dr Merrick. Dr Merrick was a good friend, and would chat to Mummy. He was never in a hurry, even when his waiting room was full of people. After you had opened your mouth and said 'aah!' he would go into the tiny dispensary which opened off his room, which was full of bottles and pill boxes and mix you a bottle. It was usually dark pink, and had a familiar peppermint flavour which was not unpleasant.

There was a lot of discussion about my adenoids being a problem again. They shouldn't have been a problem because they shouldn't have been there at all. They had been removed, together with my tonsils, when I was three. There had never been anything the matter with my tonsils but, in the 1930's, any excuse to get rid of tonsils was seized upon with alacrity. And going to the theatre to have your adenoids removed was a very good excuse. Two operations for the price of one! Mr McKinnon, who had performed the operation when I was three was to be consulted again. So we all went off to see him in Rodney Street in Liverpool. His surgery was huge - much bigger than Dr Merrick's. As instructed, I opened my mouth wide, as he held my tongue down with a spatula and shone his torch down my throat.

Mr McKinnon was effusive in his praise because I had been so good. I wondered what I had done to deserve such a compliment. After all, I had only opened my mouth. In retrospect, I wonder whether he had a guilty conscience about the lack of success he had had in curing my adenoid problem three years earlier. The only thing to do, he said, was to try again. The adenoids, he claimed, had regrown since the last operation.

Going into hospital was quite exciting. I was sorry, though, that I was to have a room to myself. I would have liked to have had some company. Pictures in books of children in hospital showed a row of beds in a long ward. This time Mummy went home and left me. The first time, when I was three, Nana had insisted that she stay by my bedside all night. The night Sister, taking pity on her, had taken her to the Staff canteen during the night for a meal. Why, I wonder, did I tell Nana about this: it was supposed to be a secret! At six, however, even Nana had to agree that I was old enough to be left alone.

I had books to read, was quite happy, and wasn't at all worried about the impending operation. Not, that is, until a silly nurse came to take me to the operating theatre. 'Now' she said, 'You're going to the theatre to see Mickey Mouse.' I was terrified. There must have been a mistake. I had thought I was going to the theatre to have my adenoids removed. I didn't mind that: I understood it. But Mickey Mouse? I didn't like Mickey Mouse, I never had liked him. Winnie the Pooh and his friends were all right, Mickey Mouse was not an attractive creature. He spoke with a strange accent. I don't suppose that well-meaning nurse ever realised how much she had upset me.

So we went to the theatre. It was a relief to see Mr McKinnon, and not Mickey Mouse. A large black mask was pressed over my nose so that I couldn't breathe properly and, at the same time, a huge metal clamp stretched open my mouth and hurt my teeth. Some of them were loose. I was sure they would be knocked out. I woke up in bed. It was all over. But I did have earache. I slept.

When I woke up again a nurse brought a tray in with some dinner on a plate. I didn't want it. I didn't tell her that I didn't want it. If she brought it to me, that meant I was supposed to eat it, whether I wanted it or not. The stew and the potatoes were not too much of a problem, though my teeth were a bit wobbly for chewing. But there were butter beans on the plate, too. I hated butter beans. I still do. I managed to push a few down, mixing them up with gravy. Then I was sick. All over the bed. All over the tray. I rang my bell, and the nurse came back. I expected her to be cross, and was surprised when she was quite understanding. She took away the tray, and changed my nightie and the sheets.

When it was time to go home Daddy brought the car to the front door of the hospital. I got in the back. And on the seat was a box. Through the cellophane inset I could see that it was a new doll. She was dressed in blue, and I called her Betsy. I didn't know what I had done to deserve a present, and it wasn't my birthday, but I took Betsy out of the box and cuddled her all the way home. She was a lovely doll.

So I had finally got rid of my adenoids. But I still had earache. When I complained about aches and pains there was a different reaction from Mummy, Daddy and Nana. Mummy tried to persuade me that it wasn't as bad as I thought. If I went away and played I would soon forget about it. Headaches she would not tolerate. Only adults had headaches, never children. Anyone thinking they might have a headache was sent out to walk round the outside of the house three times, breathing in the fresh air. The same remedy was meted out to anyone looking a bit pale. Daddy would respond by using a special voice, looking worried, and wondering if we should send for Dr Merrick. I didn't like the fuss he made, Mummy was much more reassuring. Nana reacted by going to her medicine cupboard to try out one of her favourite remedies. Tummy ache was not a complaint to confess to readily. The treatment was not pleasant: a mustard plaster slapped over the navel, and a dose of syrup of figs at bedtime. For earache Nana warmed some olive oil in a teaspoon, and tipped it in the offending ear. Most of it ran down my neck. Then she warmed a piece of cotton wool and stuffed that in my ear. It was like wearing earplugs. I couldn't hear.

The earache got worse, and my neck swelled up on the left side, so that I couldn't move my head. Nana made a poultice of antiphlogistine and wound it round my neck like a scarf. Every morning and every evening, she heated the antiphlogistine, which came in a tin, in boiling water, then spread the thick, hot, grey paste on a piece of muslin with a knife. It was slapped onto my neck while it was still very hot, and it brought tears to my eyes. Mummy tried to clean out the thick, yellow discharge from my left ear as, despite the great wad of cotton wool, it was making yellow stripes on her white pillow slips. I resisted. It hurt too much. I cried. So Dr Merrick came.

Dr Merrick managed to clean my ear without hurting too much, and he came every day for weeks on end to do it. But the earache didn't get better. One day he came with some very good news. There were some new tablets, called "M and B," which were reputed to act like magic on infections such as mine. They were, I think, one of the very first antibiotics. 'Good' said Mummy, 'We'll try anything.' 'No' said Nana, 'You're not experimenting on this child.' There was an argument. Mummy won. The tablets were crushed between two spoons, mixed with water, and I swallowed them. Dr Merrick was right. The gooey yellow discharge dried up. The swelling in my neck subsided. But there were so many scars on my left eardrum that that ear has been pretty useless as an instrument of hearing ever since.

I had been away from school for seven weeks. I wasn't in "Transition" now, I was in "Prep B. " And the Form Mistress was Miss Headridge. Everyone else had had a chance to get used to Prep B, and to Miss Headridge. Prep B's Form room wasn't in North Block, it was in South Block, up the stairs, on the balcony floor. And in Prep B everyone wore uniform. I had a pale green blouse, a green and blue tie with horizontal stripes, a navy blue gymslip, a navy blue gabardine raincoat and a navy felt hat with a green hatband which had a "C" for Cowley on the front. I was proud of my new uniform, but I was a bit nervous about going back to school. Mummy went with me to the door of the Form room. Everyone stared at me. I felt like a stranger.

This was the room in which, for the first time in my life, I experienced boredom. And I found it extremely disconcerting. There were about twelve sums on the blackboard. They were "tens and units," all low numbers, to be multiplied by two. There was not even the challenge of dealing with "carrying" numbers. I completed those sums in about three minutes, and put up my hand. I thought Miss Headridge would be pleased. She wasn't. I must wait. I must wait until everyone else had finished. Why were some people so slow? I waited and waited. My legs ached. My feet prickled. I fidgetted. Miss Headridge was helping the slow ones, but she was ignoring the quick ones. I longed for some more sums - harder ones, or a book to read. This was boredom. It was painful. I day-dreamed. This could have been when day-dreaming became an unfortunate habit. That, together with my defective hearing and Miss Headridge's quiet voice, did not augur well for my progress in Prep B.

I don't think Miss Headridge and I ever got on too well together. There was one time when I apparently behaved very strangely. And nobody understood. The school was collecting unwanted toys for refugees. We did a lot for refugees in 1938 and 1939. I took 3d to school each Monday morning for the "Refugee Fund." And now they needed some toys. I didn't mind parting with toys. I had plenty to spare. But I knew what would happen if Mummy heard about the collection. Although everyone else was bringing in one teddy or doll or game or puzzle, if I told Mummy we were collecting toys, she would fill the big blue suitcase and take that to school. I appreciated her thought. I was quite prepared to be generous. But I didn't want to be different from the other children. So I didn't even mention the toy collection at home. Miss Headridge couldn't understand why I didn't make a contribution. When she told Mummy this, Mummy couldn't understand either. So the next morning she carried the suitcase full of toys right to the Form room door, and embarrassed me in front of my friends. I suppose it served me right!

My long absence from Prep B had resulted in a further problem. A strange new area of school work known as "English" had commenced, and by the time I joined the Form a new language was in use. "Nouns," "verbs," "adjectives" and "adverbs" were confusing new terms. Writing, which I had enjoyed with Miss Fitch, had developed complications in my absence. One day we were asked to write a "paragraph" at home on a particular subject.

Reluctant to reveal my ignorance at not knowing what a paragraph was, I wondered if Mummy could help? I had my sheet of paper and guessed that a paragraph was probably something to do with how much writing appeared on it. 'How long is a paragraph?' I asked. 'It can be long or short: as long as you like' was the accurate but unhelpful reply. 'Is it the same as a page?' I asked. 'I've told you, as long as you like. ' No further help was forthcoming. Children would get more useful answers to their questions if they would only ask the right questions! I don't remember how much I wrote, or whether my work was acceptable to Miss Headridge. Nor do I remember how long it was before I discovered what the word "paragraph" meant. But I do know that English as a school subject remained one area of school work in which I always lacked confidence.

Pre-War Holidays

'Now we'll put everything in the cases' Mummy would say each year, 'We won't take any carrier bags.' And each year, after we had stowed everything in the cases, sat on the lids to close them, and heard the metal fasteners give a satisfying click, we would find several "last minute" items which had to be stuffed into brown paper carrier bags with string handles. We did the packing on Saturday morning. Daddy and Nana finished work at dinner time on Saturdays. After dinner we loaded the car, strapping the cases onto the outside luggage rack. The black soft-topped case had to come inside. We sat on the travelling rugs with the buckets and spades at our feet. It was a very exciting time. Arriving at our destination was exciting, too, but I didn't always enjoy the bit in between. Often I felt sick, and sometimes we had to stop by the roadside while I was sick.

The annual two week Summer holiday was always spent at the seaside, at a busy resort. My Father had had enough of quiet country holidays when he had been taken to Scotland as a boy. What a pity this was, for his family came from a beautiful area of Perthshire! There is a photograph of him, with his mother, father and sister, sitting on the rocks beside the river in the Pass of Killiekrankie. He looks about seven years old. He must have been too young to appreciate the scenery, and certainly he couldn't have played in the river in the clothes he was wearing at the time. His Scottish holidays had been boring, and he sought the greatest contrast he could for his own children: fairgrounds, swimming pools, busy hotels, bustling seaside piers and seasonal variety shows. So I was grown up before I discovered the attractions of the land of my Menzies' forebears, as I was never taken there as a child. Now I holiday in Scotland every year!

When I was five we had a holiday at Cleveleys. This holiday was memorable because of the disappointment at finding nuts in my prize lollipop. It was a prize for going onto the stage and singing "On the good ship Lollipop". I suppose I imagined myself as a second Shirley Temple! It must have been painful for the adults watching, as I know I couldn't sing in tune. The stage was in the open air, on the promenade. It was a wooden affair with a striped canvas awning. It was a sort of Pierrot Show, and I didn't hesitate when the pierrot with the red bobble on his conical hat invited would-be child entertainers onto the stage. The audience clapped politely, and I was handed my reward. It was a huge lollipop, as big as a teaplate. It was a dark rusty brown colour, and it had lots of nuts in it. I didn't like nuts. No-one else wanted it either, so we had to throw it away.

Rhos-on-Sea was another resort we liked. Alongside the Rhos Abbey Hotel was a magnificent open-air swimming pool. There was a small shallow paddling pool beside the large pool. Nana undressed us beside the pool, then sat in her deck chair as we splashed about in the sunshine. The sun was always shining, and I never remember being cold as I played for hours in my striped swimsuit and too large rubber cap, which came well down to protect my delicate ears. It must have been quite warm, but I never remember Nana discarding either her coat or her hat. Daddy was a good swimmer but, although Mummy could swim, I don't think she was ever very keen. Often she would sit in a deck chair beside Nana.

St Annes was near enough for a day trip, though we did occasionally stay here for short holidays. Again, the swimming pool was the main attraction. Like the one at Southport, this pool was filled with sea water, so it was salty. It had one edge where the water was only ankle deep. My method of getting used to the freezing cold water was to move from shallow water to deeper very, very slowly. Although the water was extremely cold in the pool at St Annes, we must have been there on some very hot days, for I remember a lovely sun-bathing area where you could stretch out on your towel and bake in the warm sunshine.

Scarborough was our favourite holiday destination, and we visited it more often than any other place. We stayed in an hotel called the "Wessex" high up on the South Shore. When we were small the beach was the most popular attraction. It was reached by a path which zig-zagged down the cliff through trees. As we walked down we caught glimpses of delights to come, and became more and more excited. On arrival, the first task was to secure three deck chairs and then choose our patch of sand. The sand was always clean, and early in the morning it would be smooth, too - just begging to be decorated with castles and pies. The deck chairs cost 4d each, and we had the shilling ready for when the attendant came round with his ticket machine. When it wasn't warm enough to change into a swimsuit we tucked our cotton frocks into our knickers. There were always friends to play with on the beach. We were a sociable family, and many people booked the same hotel for the same two weeks each year. At Christmas we exchanged cards with those we had met on holiday in August.

My wooden spade was bigger than Helen's and I was very proud of it. Daddy was good at making sand castles. We dug a moat around the finished building, and made numerous trips to the water's edge to fill our tin buckets and tip them into the moat. But by the time we came back with the second supply of water, the first had always disappeared. It was very frustrating. Sometimes we had packets of paper flags, and could decorate our castle. Sometimes we made a boat instead, or a car. We made seats in these, and went for imaginary "sails" or "rides." After a time the damp sand would dry out, and we watched sadly as all our efforts collapsed. Undeterred, there was another day tomorrow to start all over again. Maybe tomorrow's building would last a bit longer? But it never did.

Sometimes Daddy took us to the beach while Mummy and Nana went to the shops, then we met back at the hotel at lunchtime. If you were tired, you could ride up to the cliff-top in a lift. The hotel served three cooked meals a day, and the lunch as well as the dinner was a three or four course feast. Afternoon tea was substantial, too, with sandwiches, bread and butter, jam, scones, cakes and tea. We children didn't have dinner. We knew the Staff of this hotel well, as Mummy and Daddy had been coming since before we were born. The Staff never seemed to change in those days, and we would greet the waitress and the chambermaid like long lost friends. There was always a willing volunteer to babysit if the grown-ups wanted to go to a Show in the evening.

There were donkeys on the beach, and a Punch and Judy Show. We always had a donkey ride: it was a sort of ritual, and it was expected that you would endure it, even if you didn't enjoy it. And I didn't like it. The donkeys were smelly, and their backs were uncomfortable. The pommels at the front of the saddles did not offer a great deal of security. I was always relieved to get off the donkey's back. Neither did I enjoy the Punch and Judy Show. But I always watched it. Punch was very cruel. I didn't mind it when he knocked the sausages about, but I didn't think he should knock his wife about. It was even worse when he started to ill-treat the baby! Everyone laughed. I wondered why. It wasn't funny.

There was a beach hut where we went for a tray of tea. The tea came in a jug, with the milk and sugar already in it, and we asked for four cups and saucers. I always had a cup of tea. Helen didn't usually want one, but if she did she used my cup when I had finished. Then we took the tray back to the hut, and our deposit was refunded. Sometimes the ice cream man pedalled along the beach on his tricycle. Helen and I had cornets, but the grown-ups preferred wafers. If we got sticky we went down to the sea to wash our hands. The nearer you got to the sea, the wetter the sand, and the deeper the ridges on it. These hurt your bare feet, and could even be felt through rubber paddling shoes. I didn't like these. They tended to fill up with water and sand, and squash your toes. But at least the sea was in walking distance at Scarborough. At Southport it was usually so far away that you couldn't even see it.

I think we were in Ainsdale when I discovered that I didn't like marmite. We were staying in a house, not an hotel. I think we may have been taken for some sea air after one of our many childhood illnesses. Daddy and Nana must have been working, because they only came at the weekend. The house was dark, and had a long passage down to the kitchen. As guests we hadn't seen the kitchen until the day that our landlady decided that Mummy could go shopping, and that she would give us our tea with her own children. We sat on a long wooden settle facing the huge black kitchen range. A striped tablecloth covered the chenille one on the kitchen table. On the table was a plate of sandwiches. I took one and bit it, Ugh! I had never tasted anything so horrible. Whatever could I do? I decided to eat very, very slowly, and hope that no-one would notice that the sandwich I was eating at the end of the meal was the same one that I was eating at the beginning. But I think our landlady did notice, and I made myself scarce when I heard her discussing faddy eaters with Mummy! It was years later that I again tasted that same horrible sandwich filling, and learned that it was called "marmite". At least knowing its name helped me to avoid it in future when I was given a choice of sandwiches!

It wasn't very warm at Ainsdale. Each day we walked down to the beach, pushing Helen's push-chair. Sometimes we turned it round so that she was facing us instead of where we were going, to avoid the sand blowing into her eyes. The nearer you got to the beach at Ainsdale, the pinker the pavement became, and by the time you were nearly there it was covered in sand. I suppose the chilly sea breezes could be described as "invigorating." I hope they did us good!

It was always a great thrill to go and stay at Uncle Sidney's farm near St Asaph. On the way we stopped at "The Singing Kettle" for tea. You could see the huge brass kettle which hung outside the cafe from a great distance.

Helen and Barbara with cousin Stanford in the fields at "Bryntirion".

I always chose poached egg on toast. On the neat square of thin toast lay a perfectly round egg, and the edges of the plate were decorated with four small triangles of extra toast. Soon we would start to look out for the sign to "Rhualt". Then we would turn left and climb up the hill to 'Bryntirion." Mrs Jones was the housekeeper, and she and her husband looked after the house when Uncle Sidney was not there. She always gave us a warm welcome, and I was fascinated by her Welsh accent.

When the oil lamps were lit in the evening they gave a comforting glow and a warm smell. We children never missed the modern conveniences we had at home. It was a delight to run up the lane with Stanford and play hide and seek in the fields among the crops. I'm surprised that this was allowed: we must have caused quite a lot of damage.

Saturday afternoon trips to Southport continued, but now that Helen was getting bigger, Daddy usually took Helen and me to "Peter Pan's

Pool" while Mummy and Nana did the shopping. Peter Pan's Pool wasn't a pool, it was a children's fairground. Our favourite ride was on the aeroplanes. They went really high, and sometimes we stayed on for a second turn. The "Noah's Ark" was rather tame. You chose your pair of wooden animals which were joined together with a wooden seat. The animals chugged slowly round the track. Daddy would come with us in the drums. These were circular metal containers with seats around the edge. As they progressed along their rails they would turn sharply, first one way and then the other. Sometimes you would be dizzy when you got out of the drums.

We always enjoyed a ride on the Lakeside Miniature Railway. We bought return tickets and stayed on the train till it arrived back at Peter Pan's Pool. After a busy afternoon, we walked back into Lord Street, often all the way down to Woodhead's Café to meet Mummy and Nana for tea. I liked Woodheads, because it was painted in my favourite shade of pale green. The waitresses wore pale green dresses under their white aprons, too. They looked much more cheerful than the black ones worn by the waitresses at Bobby's.

When we went to Blackpool we visited the Miners' Convalescent Home way up on the breezy North Shore. This huge establishment was run by our friends, Mr and Mrs Whittaker Wood. They had two little boys, and it was fun to run with them up and down the long corridors. The rooms were immense, and we had tea in the biggest lounge I had ever seen.

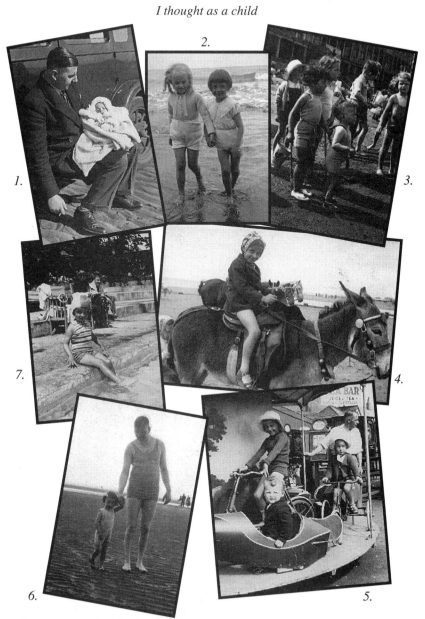

(Clockwise from top left) 1. We were taken to Southport from a very early age. 2. Barbara and a friend: we tucked our dresses into our knickers. 3. Barbara holding tightly to Helen as we watched cruel Mr. Punch. 4. The obligatory donkey ride. 5. Our seaside holidays featured fairgrounds. 6. Barbara going down to the sea with Daddy. 6. The swimming pool alongside the Rhos Abbey Hotel: my delicate ears protected by an over-large swimming cap.

Aged 7,
Getting ready for war
and a new baby

It was because of the crack in Rosemary's side that I remember my seventh birthday so clearly. From the shape of the box inside Nana's parcel I guessed that her present was another new doll. I loved dolls, but opened this box with mixed feelings. Betsy was still quite new. Would I be able to love them both equally, so that the new one would feel accepted and that Betsy would not feel neglected? No mother with a second baby could have appreciated the problem more than me. This doll was very beautiful. She was dressed in yellow. 'Her name' said Nana 'is Rosemary'. Oh dear! A lovely doll with a terrible name. I did wish her name wasn't Rosemary.

After dinner we got ready for the party. The guests were already arriving. In excitement, I dashed down the stairs with Rosemary, and she slipped out of my arms and crashed onto the hall floor. I wept. We undressed her, and discovered a huge crack right down her left side. Mummy got some sticking plaster and wound it round her tummy, I dressed her again. We took the children into the lounge and played some games. It was difficult for me to concentrate on these, because Rosemary was sitting in a chair feeling sorry for herself, and I hadn't looked after her properly. Then the conjuror arrived. We sat on the floor and watched him. He was a clever conjuror and I helped him with some of his tricks. But I didn't like magic very much, and was quite glad when it was all over.

Rosemary was the last doll I had. I played with her until I was much too old to play with dolls. That Christmas Mummy made her a beautiful new set of clothes. Every time I undressed her I saw the two strips of pink sticking plaster, and was again filled with remorse about dropping her when she was new. I think I loved her more because she was injured. I never liked her name, but by the time I was old enough to realise that I could change it I was also old enough to know that I mustn't upset Nana, who had probably chosen the name in the first place.

I don't think Mummy told anyone that there was another baby on the way until after Christmas. As a seven year old growing up fast, I sensed the unease in the house as 1939 dawned. The joy of the new baby was overshadowed by the threat of war. No-one tried to explain to me either what war was or where the baby was to come from. But I was fully aware of the practical preparations for both events.

We boiled two dozen terry nappies and two dozen muslin nappies, and hung them on the line to dry. Then we folded them and stacked them on the slatted shelves in the airing cupboard. The sewing machine was busy. Mummy cut out and sewed six long day gowns and six long night gowns. Both were embroidered, but the day gowns were smocked as well. There were long cotton petticoats, too, with ribbon threaded through the neck. Nana knitted tiny matinee jackets, and the plain centres of two large fine woollen shawls. Then Mummy knitted the delicate lacy edging on these. I held out my arms until they ached, to stretch the hanks of wool while Nana wound them into neat balls.

In contrast to the white baby clothes, Mummy was also sewing some heavy black material for the "blackout." We had to make sure that no light shone from the windows at night when the war began, in case our houses were spotted by German war planes. So all the thin curtains must be lined. There was an additional problem with the blackout at Cranley. We had many windows which weren't suitable for curtains. The stained glass window on the half-landing would be difficult to black out, as would the two small stained glass windows at either side of the fireplace in the lounge and the main bedroom. And the frosted windows in the bathroom and the lavatory didn't have curtains, either. The carpenter from Bishop's came to measure all these windows and promised to make some plywood covers for them. But either he was very slow or he was very busy, because the wooden covers didn't appear for a very long time.

They still hadn't arrived when we started to have "practice blackouts." This didn't matter much, because the evenings were light, and we were all in bed by the time it was totally dark. And perhaps the police and the wardens didn't get as far as the end of Eaton Road on their patrols. That is, until the night of July 13th/14th. This was the night of the last practice blackout before the war actually started. Helen and I were in bed and asleep, but everyone else was awake, because John was about to be born. Dr Merrick was there, and so was Nurse Dorothy Davies. All the lights were on. A policeman rang the front door bell. Did we know that our house was shining like a beacon, and could be seen from Rainford Road? We did, and my father explained about the imminent birth. The policeman was invited in for a drink. Drinking on duty was not usually allowed, but this was a special occasion.

The next morning Nana brought in the tea. July 14th, she said, was baby John's birthday. And baby John was our brother. We had to be very quiet, because Mummy was asleep. Nurse Dorothy Davies brought in the new baby. He was wrapped in a pure white shawl. He was red: his face was red and his hair was red, and I couldn't see any more of him. She put him in my bed so that I could hold him for a minute. Then she took him away. I loved him very much.

Dorothy Davies lived with us for four weeks. Mummy was supposed to stay in bed for two weeks, but she had to get up long before that to try to settle the arguments in the kitchen. We had an elderly maid called Lily at the time who thought that Dorothy Davies was too bossy. I thought so, too. She wore a navy blue long sleeved dress with a black belt and a silver buckle. Perhaps her uniform made her feel important? Her job was to look after Mummy and John. Everyone else's job was to look after Dorothy Davies. We even had to do her washing for her, and she expected her meals to be ready "on the dot".

One day we were having tea in the lounge: Dorothy Davies, Helen and me. Mummy was still in bed. Daddy and Nana were still at work. We were eating sliced bananas with sugar and cream. I had been thinking about recent events, and sorting out a few crucial questions in my mind. This seemed an appropriate moment to check a conclusion which I felt would resolve a tricky problem. 'I know' I announced without warning 'where babies come from!' Then, looking at Dorothy Davies for confirmation, I continued 'They come out of their Mummy's tummies. ' Dorothy Davies stood up. Her silver buckle was opposite my eyes, and I could tell without looking at her face that she was very cross. 'Barbara' she said, quietly and very firmly 'that is an extremely naughty thing to say - and in front of Helen, too!' I looked at Helen. She was eating her banana, and didn't seem interested in our conversation. 'Don't ever, ever say anything like that again'. And I didn't. Ever. I don't know how I finished that banana, my throat and my eyes were stinging so much. At the earliest opportunity, I escaped to the nursery, and hid there for a very long time. I wondered if I would be in trouble again, when Mummy heard of my crime. And she surely would hear, because Dorothy Davies was a renowned tale teller. Much to my relief, no-one mentioned the matter again. Perhaps everyone else soon forgot the episode. But I didn't.

It was a relief to the whole household when Dorothy Davies went home. After she left I enjoyed helping Mummy to bath baby John in his little papier mache baby bath on its pale blue metal stand. It was quite a shock to discover the difference between little boys and little girls. Up till then, when asked the difference, I would have said that boys wore shorts and girls wore frocks. One day John wee'd in the bath and it shot up right over the side. We laughed about it, and I went downstairs to fetch the floorcloth.

We were getting used to the air raid siren by now, because it was often practising. It was a very loud noise, and I sometimes wondered why it didn't wake John up when he was asleep. It never did. It must have been a normal part of his everyday life. He was a real "war baby."

John was christened on September 3rd, 1939:
the day war broke out.

Dorothy Davies was coming back for John's Christening, because she was going to be his Godmother. John was six weeks old. After he had worn his Christening gown on September 3rd he would be "shortened." All his long day gowns would be discarded, and he would wear little suits, the tiny shorts buttoned at the waist onto the little blouse tops.

We were all in the lounge listening to the wireless. The slow, solemn voice told us that the war had begun. It wasn't a surprise - we had been getting ready for a very long time. We listened in silence. Even Helen was quiet, though she couldn't have understood what was happening. After dinner we went to Church for the baptism. As soon as the Christening party arrived back from Church we turned on the wireless again. This time we were listening to the King's voice. His slow speech with its distinctive occasional hesitation added to the solemnity of the occasion. When he had finished talking there was an impressive roll of drums, and an orchestra began to play "God save the King". The Christening cake stood in the centre of the table. The lounge was full of family and friends. We all stood up in silence. Then, when the National Anthem had finished, we cut the Christening cake.

On the morning of September 4th I went outside. I wanted to know what war was like. But nothing had changed. Between our house and Wilde's, in Eaton Road, there was a plot of waste land. On this land was a little hill. I stood on the hill, and looked up into the sky. I couldn't even see or hear any aeroplanes. It was a bit of an anti-climax. Could this really be war?

We all had to go down to a house in Boundary Road to get our gas masks. I think we may have got our identity cards at the same time. It was a corner house, and the windows had been painted over. This was even worse than blackout curtains! The front room of the house had no carpet, just bare boards. There was a trestle table, where people sat behind stacks of paper, and looked very busy. And there were some wooden benches like Church pews. We sat on a pew while we queued. We queued patiently for a very long time. I don't expect anyone there at the time realised that waiting in long queues was to be a regular feature of our lives for several years to come! Having been allocated our identity numbers, we queued again for our gas masks. These were in the next room. We had to try them on. It was like the mask in the operating theatre at the hospital. I couldn't breathe. It was hot. And I couldn't see, because the visor had steamed up. There was a horrible smell of new rubber. It was very frightening. My gas mask was black, but Helen had a Mickey Mouse one. John's gas mask had to be ordered. It would be delivered in a few days time. We went home carrying our cardboard boxes, with their cords to hang round our necks. We hung them up on the pegs in the cloakroom.

I could hardly believe it when John's gas mask arrived. It was huge! We unpacked it from its box and laid the ugly, unwieldy object on the chesterfield in the sitting room. We lifted the lid, and laid our precious baby inside. It was a see-through lid, but I begged Mummy not to close it. I was sure John would not be able to breathe inside his terrifying strange capsule. She read the instructions, and said that we would have to try them out, but would wait until Daddy got home. I worried all day. We only shut John in for a few seconds. As soon as the lid was closed Mummy had to pump air in with a rubber hand pump connected to the end of the capsule. If you stopped pumping, your baby would suffocate. I don't think John ever went inside his baby gas mask again. As soon as he was big enough he had a Mickey Mouse one. And then Helen was old enough to have a grown up one like mine.

We all went into town one day to join another queue. This one was in the Windle Pilkington School, where the Ministry of Food had requisitioned a couple of classrooms. More trestle tables. More wooden benches. More long, patient waiting. But we chatted to other people while we waited. In queues, complete strangers became good friends. We were all in the same boat. I don't think anyone complained, in fact I can remember quite a lot of laughter. If anyone had a fractious baby, or an invalid at home who mustn't be left for too long, we were more than happy for them to move to the head of the queue.

At the trestle table you gave your identity number. I told the lady mine - NOAE 390/3. She was pleased that I knew it by heart already. Names, addresses and identity numbers were written on the front of our ration books. Mummy, Daddy, and Nana had buff coloured books, mine was blue. Under 5's had green books. Helen may have had a green one for a short time, but by the time rationing came into force, in January 1940, she had had her fifth birthday, and would be entitled to a blue one like me. The main advantage of a green book was that when oranges were available, a green book would entitle you to have one. With a green book you got less of some things, like meat, but more of others, like milk. You also got bottles of concentrated orange juice and bottles of cod liver oil. And not even those with green books could have a banana. The ships that used to bring the bananas to this country would be engaged in fighting the war. John would be nearly six by the time he had the opportunity of tasting a banana, and the rest of us would have almost forgotten what bananas tasted like!

We took our ration books to Marfords, and registered with Mr Foggett for our groceries. He stamped our books, and would be entitled to supply our weekly ration. No other shop would be allowed to sell us any groceries. Then we took our books into town, to have them stamped by Mr Litherland at his butcher's stall in the market. Groceries were allocated by weight, meat by cost. If you bought cheaper cuts of meat, you got more meat.

In September, 1939 Helen was due to start school. But schools couldn't open until they had enough air raid shelters to accommodate all their pupils. I was able to return to school after a couple of weeks, but Helen didn't start until after half term. Miss Headridge was my form mistress for another year, though we were in Prep A now, and had moved to the classroom opposite the science laboratory. We spent the first few days practising marching down into the basement cloakrooms. It was a long way, and we would have to try to get there before the siren stopped wailing. But I was proud to be in Prep A. It sounded very grown up. I went to school and came home by myself now with my gas mask over my shoulder. Its cardboard box had been discarded, as Nana had bought us brown canvas cases with canvas straps. One day I was walking home from school, and was nearly at the top of Kingsley Road. Elizabeth Wilde was just arriving home at the same time. She went to Cowley, too, but was a very big girl, nearly grown up. 'Which Form are you in now?' she asked. It made me feel very important to be able to say 'Prep A!'

The ritual which we performed at school every year at 11 am on the 11th November took on a particular significance in 1939. Each year we stood in silence in the aisles between the rows of desks for two minutes, then whoever was teaching us would say a prayer for all those who had lost their lives in the First World War. Now we had also to remember those who were suffering in the current conflict. It was a very solemn moment. We knew that the whole country was quiet and still for those two minutes. Even the traffic ground to a halt.

At home we soon got tired of going into our shelter when the siren went. Nothing ever happened, and it seemed a waste of time. The loggia had been turned into an air raid shelter, and its open sides had now been bricked in. There was a "blast wall" covering the French window into the lounge. All round the outside of the house, and about a foot away from the wall, sand bags were stacked to window ledge height. They provided a wonderful secret passageway for games of hide and seek. But they didn't protect the windows, so I wonder how much use they would have been in case of a bomb blast?

Daddy was packing his bags. We knew his "call-up" papers would come early, because he had been a member of the Territorial Army. The weather in the New Year of 1940 was terrible. The snow was as deep as the sand bags. But Lily was strong. We were full of admiration, as she dug a channel through the snow down to the gate. At last we were able to get through to go to school. Nana was able to go back to work. And Daddy went off to the station to catch his train to Catterick Camp in Yorkshire. He was to be a Second Lieutenant in the Royal Artillery.

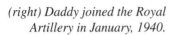

(left) The open sides of the loggia were bricked in and used as an air raid shelter. They remained "bricked in" for many years.

(right) Daddy joined the Royal Artillery in January, 1940.

Auntie Marjorie

It was Summertime, and we were having tea in the garden at "Windyridge", Momma and Dadda Toddy's house. Nowhere else in the world did I feel so safe, so secure. It was the happiest garden in the world. Any problems or worries that I brought with me disappeared as soon as I was on the garden side of the thick, dark green holly hedge. Immediately I was enveloped in the gentle, unhurried, peaceful atmosphere of the croquet lawn. Auntie Marjorie carried out the laden tea tray. I followed her. I adored her, and would have followed her to the ends of the earth. She was Mummy's best friend, and always a second Mother to me. She still is. She is my Godmother, too.

Momma and Dadda Toddy were Auntie Marjorie's parents, and were like a third set of Grandparents to me. Sometimes I watched Momma Toddy baking in her warm, friendly kitchen. She was such a relaxed sort of person that she even sat down when she was rolling out pastry! Sometimes there was a strange smell, because she used to boil the potato peelings to feed the hens. Dadda Toddy liked all kinds of birds, and he kept hens. I wasn't very keen on his hens. But I loved his "plantation." This was a patch of ground between the lawn and the cemetery railings. The grass was long and there were lots of trees. In the Spring there were daffodils and celandine. Then there were bluebells. In Summer Dadda Toddy cut down the long grass with his scythe. I watched him, then helped to gather the loose grass into a pile. He didn't mind if I jumped on the

77

piles of grass, even if I scattered it far and wide. He was never in too much of a hurry to listen to my childish chatter, and I think I told him all my secrets. When I went into the bathroom at "Windyridge" I gazed in admiration at the brown leather "strop" which hung on the wall. I was told that Dadda Toddy used it to sharpen his cutthroat razor before he shaved.

During the war Dadda Toddy often let us have eggs "off the ration", and we always carried our bucket of vegetable peelings down Eaton Road to be boiled to feed his hens. If there were plenty of eggs we would "put them down" to preserve them for later use. This procedure involved the "crock" which was kept under the stairs at Cranley. It was a large brown bowl with a creamy coloured inside, and was filled with a thin jelly-like substance called, I think, "isinglass." The eggs had first to be washed and dried, because sometimes there was straw from the hen house still sticking to them. Then we laid them carefully in the crock. Nana strove to keep a

(left) I loved Dadda Toddy and told him all my secrets.
(right) Auntie Marjorie with baby Barbara at "Windyridge".

record in her notebook of how many eggs we had left in the crock. She did her sums as eggs were added or removed, but as we often needed an egg when she was at work, I'm not sure that her calculations were very accurate! At one time there must have been two crocks, for in one of Nana's notebooks it is recorded that there were 119 eggs in the large one, and 60 in the small one: what a huge supply of eggs! I always hoped I wouldn't be asked to fetch an egg from under the stairs. It was creepy in there, and cold and damp. It was a good place for growing mould, for breeding spiders and for preserving eggs.

Mummy had a wide circle of good friends, with whom she was on Christian name terms. Some had been schoolfriends, and many she had known since her youth. As we children got to know them, too, they became "Aunties" and "Uncles". It was unheard of at the time for a child to address an adult who was not a servant by his or her Christian name. Our maids, however, whatever their age, were always referred to by their Christian names. Sometimes we went to see Sarah and Tommy in Fraser Street. I wondered why she wasn't "Auntie" Sarah, because she was grown up. Later I learned that before her marriage, she had been one of Nana's maids. So that was why Katie was never "Auntie" Katie!

Auntie Marjorie was not a relation. But she had been close to Mummy since her family moved to Hard Lane. They went to school together, and stood side by side at their Confirmation. They shared their growing-up years, organised those "subscription" dances, and were bridesmaids at one another's weddings. As Mummy was married first, I suppose she would be more accurately described as a Maid of Honour at Auntie Marjorie's wedding to Uncle Bob.

After they moved from Keswick Road, Auntie Marjorie and Uncle Bob lived at "The Grove" in Cowley Hill Lane. Their back gate opened onto "the patch" in the grounds of Cowley Girls' School. And the front of the house faced one of the entrances into Victoria Park. When we were at "The Grove" we often went for a walk in the park. We watched the men playing bowls. We fed the ducks on the duck pond. We walked round the immaculate formal gardens beside the Mansion House, and sometimes went into the museum itself. It was a bit scary, but the stuffed animals roused a sort of eerie fascination in the young children who had to stand on tiptoe to peer into the glass cases.

It was good to go to "The Grove" because, although the house itself was very different from ours, it had a familiar feel about it: the routine, the meals, the expectations - the whole regime was similar to that in our own family. And Auntie Marjorie knew without being told what we liked and what we didn't like. I think she knew me almost as well as she knew her own children, Judith and Christopher. Judith was five months younger than Helen, and Christopher was a year older than John. So I had been around longer than any of the others and, being the first baby, had undoubtably had more attention than the others.

I liked Auntie Marjorie's kitchen: it was always bright and cheerful. The pastel shades of the paintwork were calm and restful. I loved the cupboards at the side of the fireplace, especially when they were painted pale green. I remember thinking that this was a happy colour. When Mummy acquired a Summer frock in the same shade of green I was delighted. I knew she would always be happy when she wore that frock. And she was. Or perhaps it was only my own pleasure which she reflected, because I thought she never looked lovelier than when she was wearing that frock?

Birthday parties at The Grove were great fun. We played all the games which I liked. Auntie Marjorie knew them all. She knew the words of all the singing games. And as we got older she devised treasure hunts and other exciting challenges. Once I went to one of Christopher's parties. John was there too. And I was ashamed of myself. The little boys were much younger than me, and the clues for the treasure hunt were very easy. I knew the house well, and dashed around at top speed, carried away by the thrill of the game. I finished long before anyone else. I should have given the younger ones a chance. By the time I realised this it was too late, and I had won the prize. I knew I had done the wrong thing, and was very sorry. I tried to compensate by doing the only thing I could think of, I gave the prize to John.

At "The Grove" I needn't be worried about not liking anything on the tea table. I knew there would be egg sandwiches and jelly, and chocolate finger biscuits. And often I was given some of my favourite little oranges in a dish. When we had dinner at "The Grove" I could relax, too, because Auntie Marjorie liked the same things as me, and we had bread sauce with our chicken, just like we did at home.

By the time Christopher was due to start school the 1944 Education Act was on the horizon. This was a disaster for the preparatory department at Cowley Girls' School, which had admitted boys as well as girls in the first two years. Now there were to be no more admissions to the kindergarten and gradually, year by year, the Prep. Forms would disappear. Cowley was to become a Secondary Grammar School, and eventually would only admit children at the age of eleven, providing that they passed the Scholarship exam.

But Auntie Marjorie was a Froebel trained teacher of young children, so she opened her own school for Christopher and others of his age, in a large room upstairs at The Grove. That schoolroom held a fascination for me. I loved the little tables and chairs, and the low cupboards with their tiny curtains. I liked to kneel down and chalk on the low blackboard. I wanted to be a teacher of little children, too, just like Auntie Marjorie. Eventually I was, and was proud to train at the College where she had trained almost thirty years earlier.

During the war there were several occasions when we children went to stay at "The Grove". We stayed there sometimes when Nana was ill, and occasionally when Daddy had some leave he and Mummy would be able to go away for a weekend together. They knew that Auntie Marjorie would not mind having three extra children to look after, because she loved children. Weren't we lucky?

On the croquet lawn at "Windyridge". (left to right) Nana, Daddy, Dadda Toddy, Uncle Bob, Barbara, Momma Toddy, Mummy.

My friend Anne

'There's something I think I ought to tell you,' announced my friend Anne, with that "I'm dying to impress you with a devastating piece of information" look on her face. We were about seven or eight years old at the time. She had succeeded in her wish to gain my full attention. But she decided to prolong her moment of triumph. 'I'm not sure that I ought to tell you, though' she continued, contradicting her opening statement. 'It's something I heard my mother and your mother talking about, and it's about you!' I could tell from the look on her face that "it" wasn't anything designed to cheer me up.

Nevertheless, the suspense would undoubtably be as painful as whatever bombshell was about to fall. I wanted to know. But for some reason now forgotten, it was something which couldn't be told here and now. We made an appointment to meet in the Summer House at a certain time the next day. The Summer House was a popular place for discussing matters of importance which were of a secretive nature.

The hour approached. We met. I waited. 'I heard them talking and they said ...' A suitably dramatic pause accompanied the sombre expression. 'You'd better tell me' I encouraged, already going rather weak at the knees. 'They said you are going to die when you are seventy'. There it was. The secret was out. What was I to do? Such friendly sharing of confidences deserved some grateful acknowledgment. 'I'm glad you told me' I lied.

Still, my seventieth birthday was a long time away, so I had plenty of time to decide how I was going to avoid this tragedy. The problem would need to be shelved for a while, for the everyday business of living had to go on for the time being. Nevertheless, for the next couple of days, the devastating revelation about the timing of my decease constantly intruded upon mealtimes, upsetting my digestion, on schooltimes, upsetting my concentration, and on bedtimes, interrupting my sleep. When turning the matter over again in my mind while in bed one night, I hit upon a seemingly simple, pragmatic solution. On the eve of my seventieth birthday I would stay awake and pray. I would continue to pray all night. God, who was in control of life and death, liked people to pray. He certainly wouldn't let anyone die in the middle of a prayer. The solution to the problem was a great relief.

As "best friends" Anne and I often discussed serious matters such as those of birth, life and death. We also discussed the problems associated with growing up. Because Anne had an older sister she was more knowledgeable than me. One day, she had some startling news. When we were about fourteen or fifteen we would start to have bleeding problems which would prevent us from going swimming. This didn't make much sense to me. I had seen lots of ladies who were older than that at the swimming pool. We were both puzzled when I pointed this out to Anne.

Anne was the daughter of one of Mother's school friends. Her Mother was "Auntie" Jessie. Anne was six months younger than me, and lived in Hard Lane, at "Mayfield", number 25. Anne and I had played together since we were very small, but became close after we moved to Cranley. By this time she and I were old enough to walk along Eaton Road by ourselves to visit one another's houses. And we were often together in one house or the other. If I wanted to stay for tea at Anne's house, we would have to go and ask Mummy's permission. If Anne wanted to stay for tea at my house, we would have to go and ask Mary's permission. Mary was Auntie Jessie's maid. Auntie Jessie was often out, and Mary was left in charge.

Mary was very good to us. She cooked our tea and, when needed, was often willing to play with us. And we needed her for skipping. We skipped in Eaton Road. We had a long rope. Mary turned one end and Anne and I took turns to turn the other while the one who was free skipped. We knew all the traditional skipping rhymes, and practised the intricate steps until we perfected them. I don't think we ever got tired, and I don't ever remember Mary complaining, though her arm must have ached. Sometimes on dark evenings we skipped until it was too dark to see the rope.

Anne and I were always setting challenges for ourselves. We designed an ordered set of tests for bouncing balls against a wall. As each target was met, a new, harder one was set. We progressed from bouncing under legs to bouncing round backs to turning round before the ball returned to doing the whole sequence with two balls instead of one. The possibilities were endless and, as with skipping, we never tired of this game.

Anne had a "two-wheeler" bike when she was five, when I still had a tricycle. She rode along Eaton Road to show it to me, and I was very envious. It wasn't long before I had one, too. I didn't find balancing on my new bike nearly as easy as Anne had done, and Daddy ran up and down Eaton Road till he was breathless, holding on to the back of the saddle. There were many tears and bandaged knees before I could ride as well as Anne, but I finally mastered this difficult skill. Anne and I rode together up and down Eaton Road, and soon became adept at avoiding the potholes without losing speed. This challenge overcome, we set ourselves a new one. This was to ride as slowly as possible without falling off. I soon became skilled at this trick and later, when the slow bicycle race was included in the Cowley sports, I was invariably the winner. As I was in the skipping race.

Judith and I on our tricycles, Helen standing, and Anne with her "two wheeler".

At Anne's house there were two big attractions. One was the grand piano in the front room. The other was the car in the garage. We played duets on the piano, though neither of us had had any lessons. Uncle Albert, Anne's Father, was a good pianist. Anne and I experimented with pitch and rhythm until we achieved what, to us, was a satisfactory sound. Then we went out into the hall, re-entered the room hand in hand, bowed solemnly to an imaginary audience, perched side by side on the piano stool, and performed our latest composition. Any mistake would send us out into the hall to repeat the whole performance. Later, Anne's big sister Margaret taught us how to play "chopsticks" and we played this for hours on end.

In the garage at "Mayfield" the car was "laid up for the duration of the war". Petrol was only allowed for essential purposes, and there were very few cars to be seen on the roads. Hathaways had collected our car as soon as Daddy left to join the army. But Uncle Albert's car was in his garage, raised from the floor on wooden blocks to protect its wheels. I think the tyres were removed and stored elsewhere. The car was large, and made a fine house, or hospital, or whatever our imaginations dictated. It was very comfortable, and I loved the smell of the leather seats.

At Cranley Anne and I played similar imaginative games in the nursery. We bossed poor Helen about unmercifully. When we played "school" I think we treated her very badly. One thing we could rarely persuade her to do was to help with the tidying up. Though we resorted to bribery and other unfair devices, she inevitably disappeared and left us surrounded with all the mess. Although I always enjoyed arranging things in order, I was often defeated by the muddle in the nursery. I would start in one corner, methodically folding dolls' clothes, and tucking dolls neatly into their beds, but by the time Mummy came in to inspect the room the bit I had achieved was hardly visible amongst the rest of the jumble.

Often Mary took us for a walk round Windle Hall fields. This was a favourite route, and usually we walked up Hard Lane, past the cemetery, along Abbey Road towards Windle Hall, crossing the bridge over the East Lancashire Road, across the fields, back to Windle Island, and home along Rainford Road. Sometimes we ran on ahead in Rainford Road and hid from Mary in the concrete "pill-box" with its narrow open doorway and slit-like windows like those in the old castles in our story books. These attractive play places had been erected in 1940 after France had capitulated, and preparations were made for a threatened invasion of our country.

One day we were doing our walk the wrong way round. There was a small sweet shop in Rainford Road, opposite the smithy, and not far from Windle Island. We had a penny each to spend, so we set off along Rainford Road to go to the sweet shop at the start of our walk. In my view, sucking or chewing sweets was a very overrated pastime, but I did love a bit of chocolate. We arrived at the shop and made our choice. Anne and Helen took ages to decide. Eventually they chose their two halfpenny bags each of toffees or boiled sweets. I had my small penny bar of chocolate: that was an easy choice. Mary pointed out to me that Anne and Helen had much more for their money than I had, and did her best to persuade me to change my mind. I tried to convince her that I really did prefer the chocolate, but she insisted that I would regret my mistake.

Anne and Helen chewed and sucked all the way round Windle Hall fields. Their jaws must have been aching. I ate my chocolate in the first few minutes and enjoyed it. Throughout the whole of that walk Mary taunted me with the claim that if I had chosen more wisely my pennyworth would have lasted much longer. 'I know' I protested 'and I don't mind'. I think I remember this episode in its every detail because I was telling the truth, and here was an adult who refused to believe me.

Anne's sister Margaret had a tent. In the Summer it was pitched on the waste land which adjoined the entry at the back of the Hard Lane houses. Usually Margaret's tent was a "hospital", and she was dressed in her nurse's uniform. Sometimes her cousin Pam was with her. And sometimes Anne and I were invited in to be the patients. It smelled like a real hospital, because Margaret always managed to get hold of some real TCP. She had real bandages, too. The tent was often pitched behind Grandma Murray's house. Grandma Murray was Anne's and Margaret's grandmother, and she lived at number 7 in Hard Lane.

Sometimes on Sundays we went to tea at Grandma Murray's house. She always made potato cakes and they were delicious. In Grandma Murray's yard there was an unusual kind of swing. It was a bit like the swingboats which you saw on the fairground. Two people could sit on each side, facing one another. The swingboat was supposed to rock gently. But it didn't when we got on it. If you stood up and pushed hard with both hands and feet you could get it to rock violently and swing very fast. After tea, we dashed out to the swing. Margaret and Pam got there first, followed by Anne and Helen. I was always last. I wonder why? By the time I arrived the others would be swinging fast, would declare the swing 'full up', and wouldn't let me get on. I was always timid in face of this opposition, and was a sitting target for teasing. Usually I disappeared out of the back gate, trailed home across the field in tears, and told my sad story to anyone at home who might be willing to listen. I never got any sympathy, because I should have stood up for my rights and not been such a baby. I knew that Anne would not have behaved like this to me had she been on her own, and tended to put all the blame on Margaret and Helen, who often "ganged up" against Anne and me! Sometimes on those sorry Sundays, Anne would follow me home later, and I always forgave her.

There were two attic rooms on the second floor in Grandma Murray's house. On the first floor was a large old chest of drawers. And one of these drawers was full of dressing up clothes. In one of the attic rooms there was a table tennis table. We stood this on its side, and by carefully separating the two sections of the table about eighteen inches we had a perfect backdrop for our shows, with a central entry point for the performers. There were endless performances, usually organised by Margaret - variety shows with singing and dancing, and little one-act plays. Often I was sent home to fetch my Chinese outfits. Reflecting the mood of the war, our songs and dances became more and more patriotic. We sang 'Three cheers for the red, white and blue' as we waved our huge Union Jack. Occasionally we had an adult audience, but were often quite content just to entertain ourselves. We were an entirely female group. Barbara Murray, another of Anne's cousins, would often join us. This Barbara was one of seven in my Form at school. "Barbara" must have been a popular name at the time!

We practised for hours for one of our shows, Sunday after Sunday. Then we invited all the adults we could muster, and made a small charge for admission. We sent the proceeds to the "Spitfire fund" and, with our letter of thanks came a badge for each of us with a picture of a spitfire. We were so proud of these. I still have mine. Under the aeroplane is the word "shareholder. " It was many years after receiving the badge that I learned what a shareholder is. But I was always very proud of that badge.

Inevitably, at this time, we sometimes played "wars". But I don't think our unsuspecting "enemies" had any idea that we were at war with them. I suppose we chose Tony and Barbara Scott, who lived next door to Cranley, as enemies because they were never very friendly. We spied on them from the ditch at the bottom of the lawn. This was always a "distance" war, and I don't think we ever engaged in any close-up combat. We were a bit afraid of Mr Scott. He tended to look rather forbidding, and was never very pleasant when we plucked up courage to ask if we could retrieve our lost balls when they strayed into his garden. He would never let us in ourselves, but said he would find the ball when he had time, and throw it back. But sometimes he forgot. So we waited for him to go out, then crept gingerly through the hedge, keeping a wary eye on the Scott windows. I think he found out that we had sneaked into his garden - probably we had trampled on his precious plants, because one day he came round to complain, and this put a stop to our little adventures through the hedge. I don't think the Scotts approved of our noisy games. Tony and Barbara were very quiet. Sometimes we did invite them to come round and play, but it was never allowed. When the "Stop me and buy one" ice cream man stopped his tricycle at the gate and rang his bell we all dashed out to buy our cornets. But Tony and Barbara had to share one between them.

In the outside lavatory at Cranley, written in a childish hand with wax crayon on the bare brick wall was the crude but revealing statement: "B, H and A v Scotts, Sandbags den." It was still visible when we left Cranley in 1961.

We also played with John and Edward Jones, who lived next door to Scotts in Kingsley Road. John was six months younger than me, and Edward was a year younger than Helen. As a toddler, Edward was a "wanderer." Sometimes he took Helen with him. Annie, who was Mrs Jones's live-in maid, would often come round to see if we had seen Edward anywhere. If he couldn't be found, Anne and I would be sent out to look for him. I think Helen and Edward were about two and three years old when we found them both playing on Windle Hall bridge.

One day John Jones and I got into trouble. John had a useful wooden trolley, which we decided to turn into a mobile shop. We collected together some sweets and comics, and started to knock at the doors of our neighbours, in an attempt to sell our wares. We didn't get far. Someone informed on us, and our business initiative was brought to an abrupt halt.

We began to develop a close relationship with Mrs Jones and, a few years later, after she was widowed, she became "Auntie Maggie."

John and Irene

Irene loved John almost as much as I did. And she was like a big sister to me. She was the successor to Lily, who left us soon after John's birth, and she couldn't have been more different. She was fourteen years old, and wore white ankle socks just like me. But when she came for her interview she wore a grown-up hat! She came to us straight from school, and we paid her 6/- a week. She didn't wear uniform. I think that maids' uniforms were probably one of the unessential luxuries which disappeared when the war started. But she wore some pretty aprons, and a narrow ribbon round her dark, shoulder length hair, which was tied in a bow on the top of her head.

Irene lived at Haresfinch, in Ewart Road, and went home after tea each day. On Sunday she went home after dinner. After Irene joined us we had to have dinner earlier on Sundays, so that she wouldn't be late for Sunday School. Mummy thought she should leave as soon as she had finished washing up, but Nana insisted that she should also wash the kitchen floor when the washing up was done. Nana had lived with this Sunday ritual all her life, and was reluctant to let her standards drop. But this extra chore was often the one which caused Irene to have to run all the way along Eaton Road, down Hard Lane to the City Road end, and then all the way along Washway Lane. She must have been breathless by the time she rushed into her Sunday School! Eventually Irene was excused from the Sunday floor washing, and we even helped her with the washing up, so

Irene with John, Helen and Barbara
in the garden at Cranley

that she wouldn't be late. By this time she had almost become one of the family, and had endeared herself to us all. She was kind and helpful, always smiling, and John adored her. When she arrived in the morning she didn't take her coat off, because her first duty was to take Helen to school, and John often went too, in his pram. I didn't go with them, as by this time I had arranged either to call for Anne or to meet Barbara Murray at the top of the Green.

One day Irene had an extra trip down to school and back, because Helen had arrived home by herself, and it wasn't hometime! Miss Pearson had sent her back into the Formroom when the rest of the Form were outside. But she didn't send in the child with whom Helen had been fighting and who, by all accounts, had been equally guilty. Helen was outraged at this unfair treatment and set off for home, a journey she had not previously attempted alone. Irene was the one who had to drag her, unwillingly, back to school. Poor Irene! I think she was as upset as Helen was, particularly as Helen continually repeated her threat to blow her nose on

Miss Pearson's best coat all the way back to school. Miss Pearson was so relieved to see that Helen was safe and sound after her adventure, that there were no further recriminations. There were none at home, either, as Miss Pearson had admitted that she had been wrong to send Helen in to school alone.

John never crawled but, in a sitting position, he used one leg to propel himself along, digging his heel into the floor and wearing a hole in his soft slippers as he sped round the house at great speed. He followed Irene wherever she went, and we had no fears for his safety, knowing that she was always close beside him. Later, as his baby babbling began to resemble proper words, whenever he needed attention we would hear the familiar shout for 'I'ene!' And he would cry bitterly if she had gone home, and didn't respond.

But John didn't cry much. He was a contented baby. Soon I was big enough to take him out for walks, and it was a pleasure to push his pram. He beamed at everyone we met. I often pushed him along Rainford Road and into Bleak Hill Road, to see the cows at the farm. The farm was smelly, and I didn't think much of the cows myself, but John seemed to like them. Sometimes we stopped at the Smithy, especially if a horse was being shod. But nothing would convince me that the horse was not hurt when the nails were driven into its feet. Sometimes we walked down Gamble Avenue to Victoria Park to see the ducks. I would like to have shown him the stuffed animals, too, but I couldn't take the pram into the Mansion House. Sometimes we walked all the way round Windle Hall fields, and would stop on the bridge over the East Lancashire Road, to look down on the cars and buses. It is difficult to imagine now that we sometimes had to wait for ages before a car came along! Often we saw more aeroplanes than cars. When we heard a plane John would look upwards and point. I think he liked planes even when he was a baby in a pram. None of us suspected then that his chosen adult profession would be as an airline pilot.

For the first six years of his life John only saw his Father for the short periods when he was home on leave. We taught him to say 'Daddy,' but it was a long time before he attached this name to one particular person. From his pram he would call out 'Daddy' to any passing gentleman in khaki, much to everyone's amusement. But people understood. I don't think he was the only baby to make this mistake.

When John was a few months old the three of us went to stay with Uncle Horrie and Auntie Vie for a week. Auntie Vie was Mummy's cousin.

91

Daddy had some leave, and he and Mummy had been persuaded to go away by themselves for a change. Uncle Horrie and Auntie Vie lived in Birmingham but, because of the war, were living in their holiday cottage at Cleobury Mortimer in Shropshire. It was a lovely bungalow with a huge garden. There was a stream at the bottom of the garden, which you could cross by an interesting little narrow footbridge. Uncle Horrie had a favourite joke. Every visitor who came to his bungalow was taken down to the stream, and invited to see his "water otter". When they arrived he would pull on a string attached to the bank and up to the surface would come an old kettle! The bungalow was called "Anmerlea," and this name was devised by combining the names of Auntie Vie's three children: Leon, Mervyn and Anita.

I loved the countryside at Cleobury Mortimer, it was quiet and peaceful. This time I had been charged with looking after John. While we were at Cleobury Mortimer John was ill. Auntie Vie said he must stay in his cot until he was better. I could go out to play. No fear! Wild horses couldn't have moved me from that cotside. I had my meals there, too. Auntie Vie mixed some Benger's Food. It would do John good. He didn't want it. I talked to him, I played with him, I told him stories, I distracted him, and when he opened his mouth I popped in a spoonful of Benger's Food. It took most of the day, but he ate it all, and I was very pleased with myself. He fell asleep, and Auntie Vie thought that I, too, should go to bed. She would sleep in the room with the cot, and take care of him during the night. 'No' I said firmly, 'If he wakes up, he'll want me.' And the only bed I would sleep in was the one alongside the cot. I slept soundly, all through the night. I don't know whether John woke up or not!

John was a slippery baby and when he was old enough to go in the big bath we had to hold onto him tight. He was always slipping under the water. He had a small chair on wheels which he was always slipping out of, too. It had armrests and a tray, so he could hold on, but this didn't prevent him from disappearing under the tray and onto the floor. If we were pushing him fast, which we often did when he was in his chair out on the lawn, it was difficult to stop before we started to run over him. Sometimes we hadn't noticed that he had left the seat and was sitting on the grass. Then he would protest, and Irene would come running to the rescue. Irene must have spent many hours walking around with John clinging to her fingers as he took his first steps. He was sixteen months old before he walked unaided, and I think Irene was more proud of his achievement than anyone else. By this time she was more of a children's Nanny than a housemaid.

Irene was only with us for three years. She didn't want to go. We didn't want to lose her, but at the age of seventeen she had to register for war work, and domestic service was not a "reserved occupation" like farming and nursing. If she wasn't going into the forces, she would have to go to work in a munitions factory. She wept. So did I. John didn't understand, but we wondered what he would do without her. She would earn a lot more money in a munitions factory, but she didn't want a lot more money, she wanted to stay at Cranley. Mummy went into town to an office to plead our case with some official. But he wasn't prepared to bend the rules. Irene had to go. On her last day we gave her a sort of party, a special tea, and she ate it at the big table with us, instead of in the kitchen by herself. She clung to John, and cried miserably. She promised to come back when the war was over. But I think Mummy knew that she wouldn't do that once she was used to the increase in her wages. For a time Irene came to visit us often. And for several years we went down to Ewart Road on her birthday, August 31st, with a card and a small gift. We never forgot Irene, and I don't suppose she ever forgot John.

Helen and I pushed John around the
garden in his chair on wheels.

The War Effort

'There's nothing you can do to help' Nana said 'with a husband in the army and three small children to look after.' But Mummy insisted on going to the meeting in the Open Air School. When she came back she told us that she hadn't agreed to do firewatching, but she had offered to house a stirrup pump. We would keep it in the outside lavatory, alongside a bucket of water, and a sign could be put up at the gate to show everyone where it was kept. When it arrived we practised using it. It was fun. One end went into the bucket, you pumped hard, and directed the nozzle where you wanted to squirt the water. But I feel sure the same effect could have been achieved with less effort by simply emptying the water from the bucket directly onto the fire. When there was an air raid I sometimes wondered whether anyone would come for the stirrup pump. But they never did.

Often we were asleep when the air raid warning siren went, because most air raids were at night. Helen and I now had our beds in the nursery, and John's cot was there, too. Sometimes Nana slept with me in my bed and Mummy slept with Helen. Then we were quite near to the shelter. Mummy and Nana wearily put on their dressing gowns, and carried Helen and John through the French windows into what had formerly been the loggia. I stumbled after them, eyes heavy with sleep. It was after several consecutive nights of this performance that the beds and the cot were moved into the loggia. We all slept in our shelter for several months.

By the light of the one-bar electric fire, Mummy stood by the cot rocking John to sleep. I liked to hear her singing, but this was the only time I remember hearing her soothing singing voice: 'Go to sleep, my little piccaninny' she sang, 'Darkies will get you if you don't, Hush-a-bye, Lullaby, Mamma's little darling, Mamma's little piccaninny coo.' I don't suppose I have remembered the words correctly, but the tune has stayed in my mind for, the song ended, she would hum the tune over and over again until all three of us were asleep.

It was very quiet in the evening in the shelter. I think the blast wall must have deadened any noise from the lounge where Mummy and Nana would be sitting knitting and sewing, and listening to the wireless. Nana darned all the socks. As I lay waiting for them to come to bed I would wonder - are they still there? Suppose a bomb had dropped on the rest of the house, and only the shelter was untouched? If the three of us were left on our own, what would I do? I went hot, and my heartbeat quickened. I had to know. What excuse could I think up this time to peep into the lounge and reassure myself that all was well? Mummy knew my excuses well, and would be cross because she knew I wasn't telling the truth. So I hesitated for a long time before daring to open the door and peep through the green velvet curtains. It had to be either a drink of water, or needing the lavatory. The first was rarely allowed, because of causing the second. And you couldn't go upstairs to the lavatory in the night. So "the article" was placed just inside the door for me. And if it was still empty when I got up, I would be sent back to bed with some angry words. But I had achieved my purpose, reassured myself that Mummy and Nana were safe, and could now go to sleep. I rarely woke up when Nana came to get into the bed with me, but was comforted by her warm presence if I woke up during the night.

Sometimes we all woke up in the night. 'Bombs' said John, one of the first words he could say clearly. We sympathised with the people of Liverpool, who were undoubtably suffering a "direct hit," and were glad that we lived in St Helens. On one particularly noisy night we waited for the "all clear" then, before we went back to sleep we went upstairs to look out through the window towards Liverpool. The sky was alight. Liverpool was ablaze. The huge grey barrage balloons were silhouetted against the brilliant redness of the night sky. It was a very impressive sight. My eye took in the picture, which I have never forgotten. But, at the time, my mind did not comprehend the extent of the tragedy which it signified. Each day Nana brought home a copy of the Liverpool Echo, and perused the lengthy columns of names on the latest list of casualties.

There were a few isolated incendiary bombs which dropped on St Helens. One demolished a house in Bishop Road, and we all went down to view the damage. The one which was closest to us embedded itself in the patch of waste ground right next to the drive at Cranley. Although I believe it failed to ignite, Nana, who was unwisely standing by the open back door at the time, claimed that her leg had been grazed by a piece of shrapnel.

Gradually, wartime shortages had crept up on us. We were urged to "dig for victory". The flower beds in the back garden had disappeared. Mr Owen had planted vegetables, and in the greenhouse he was growing lettuces and tomatoes. And very good this home produce tasted, too, especially the potatoes. New, strange foodstuffs appeared. It was good to be able to get hold of a tin of spam. Spam fritters made an appetising meal. You could make the batter with dried egg. Reconstituted, dried egg really did taste like shell eggs, and I think we actually preferred it for making scrambled eggs on toast. I wasn't very keen on the concentrated orange, though. It did taste a bit like oranges, but was very strong, and when I had eaten some I could taste it for the rest of the day, It often appeared as a pudding at school, spread on a square of pastry, because of its added vitamin C. Lord Woolton, who was the Minister of Food, spoke on the wireless to tell us how to make sure that we were getting enough of all the essential vitamins. We learned a lot about vitamins from Lord Woolton.

I did understand why it was sensible to stay at school for dinner, though I didn't like it very much. If there was an air raid just as you were going home you had to wait for the "all clear" before you could leave school. There was a tin of biscuits in each of the school shelters, in case you were stuck there till teatime. If there was a air raid when you were at home, you had to wait for the "all clear" before you could set off back to school. And if you were on your way to or from school when the siren went, and a policeman or an air raid warden spotted you, you would be ushered into the nearest street shelter. One day I was nearly home. The siren went just as I was passing the side gate to Cowley Boy's School, and unfortunately I had to go into the shelter on the other side of the road. I pleaded that I could be home in a couple of minutes if I ran, but wasn't allowed to go. It was cold, dark and damp. I was squashed in at the far end. There I had to stay until either we heard the "all clear," or I was collected by an adult. Mummy guessed where I was, and came to collect me. She couldn't see me, and stood at the door shouting my name. I pushed my way through the crowd, and was rescued.

There was another good reason for having school dinners. The dinner you got at school was additional to the family's food ration. It made sense to take advantage of this. School meat was my biggest worry. It wasn't like home meat. It was hard to cut, and even harder to chew. Chewed until it turned white, it often ended up wrapped in my hanky in the small top pocket of my gym slip, because I had found it impossible to swallow. I was a very slow eater. I often sat at a table with older girls, who finished quickly. I always hoped that one of them would go and refill our water jug. More water helped the food to go down. We poured the water into our chipped and cracked mugs. But I don't think there was any danger of infection, because the water always tasted of strong disinfectant.

Why did the air raid siren always go at dinner time? We all picked up our plates and our knives and forks, and carried them down into the "dungeons". These were narrow passages in the basement of North Block, lined with wooden forms, and we sat opposite one another in long rows. We balanced our plates on our knees. I had short legs and my feet dangled several inches from the floor. My knees sloped downwards, and offered a very insecure resting place for a plate of dinner. The only way to prevent the plate from slipping down onto the concrete floor was to hold it firmly with one hand. Then I needed a hand for my knife and a hand for my fork, I didn't have enough hands! How could I eat my dinner?

Despite food shortages, we children were never hungry. I suspect that the adults in most families deprived themselves to feed their children. I don't think Daddy was ever hungry during the war. I'm sure the army was well fed. When he came home on leave he brought his emergency ration card, and Mr Foggett supplied us with an extra ration. But Daddy probably never knew that we had been saving up our bacon ration for weeks so that he could have bacon and egg for his breakfast when he came home on leave. Nana's diet was the biggest problem, She had a duodenal ulcer, and was used to having fish for her tea every day. Fish was not rationed, but was in short supply. So we had to queue for Nana's fish. Sometimes I stood in Spaven's queue while Mummy did all the rest of the shopping. And she would be quite annoyed if she came back and noticed that I had only moved up one or two places, She was right when she surmised that I must have "let people in." It was difficult to keep your place when you were only small, and grown-ups elbowed their way in front of you. It was even worse when I was told that Nana's fish was "under the counter." This meant that when Mr Spaven bent down and lifted out our parcel, already wrapped and with our name on it, some people in the queue would make rude remarks about preferential treatment. I wished I had the courage to explain about Nana's duodenal ulcer.

Officially we didn't approve of the "black market", where a privileged few were able to get extra rations. However, each Saturday afternoon we took the trolley bus down to Parr and went to Babs' shop for that very purpose. Nana convinced us that we were doing Babs a good turn as well as getting a few extras for ourselves. Babs was Katie's sister, and she and her daughter, Frances, kept a little shop on the main road just before the turning into Fraser Street. Nana knew Babs well, and often called into the shop on her way to "the Works" with some little gift for Babs' family. Some of Babs' registered customers were very poor. Often they couldn't afford to buy the whole of their grocery ration. So Babs had some groceries to spare. Our basket was taken through the curtain to the room at the back of the shop. It was returned to us covered with a teatowel. We handed over our 5/-. We never knew what was in the basket until we arrived home. It was a deadly secret, and we couldn't even have a peep on the bus. Always there would be small packets of butter, sugar and tea. Sometimes there was a bit of bacon or cheese, And if we were very lucky we might get a precious tin of fruit, or a tin of salmon.

Later there were problems with our visits to the shop. Some of Babs' customers were becoming suspicious. This might affect Babs' business. So we began to visit Sarah's house instead. Sarah and Tommy lived in Fraser Street. By Saturday afternoon the illicit goods would have been transferred from Babs' shop to Sarah's house, and the basket would be packed in Sarah's back kitchen. We handed over the 5/- to Sarah. As Helen and I got bigger Mummy persuaded us to go to Sarah's on our own. We took the basket and the tea towel, and I was charged with looking after the 5/-. I always hoped that no-one would stop us on the way, and ask us what was in the basket.

At Anne's house there were a few wartime extras, too. Uncle Albert had bought "Sharples", the shop which Dadda Toddy owned until his retirement, and, although this shop sold mainly clothing, fabrics and haberdashery, he was able, through the trade, sometimes to get 7 lb tins of half-coated chocolate biscuits. One of these tins often stood beside the kitchen cabinet at "Mayfield." Sometimes Mary would give Anne and me one each at teatime and sometimes, when no-one was looking, we would help ourselves to more than one each! They were delicious.

It wasn't only food which was in short supply. Amongst many other commodities, paper was a problem, too. When we went shopping we took used paper bags to put the new goods in. And paper in school exercise books became so thin that it was impossible to rub anything out without making a hole in the paper. If you used ink the writing would show through to the other side of the page. We wrote close to the narrow margin, and on every line. We were sent with a full exercise book to a locked office halfway up the stairs in South block. It was a tiny stockroom. Someone would come to check the book. Every page was examined. If you had left a space you were sent away to fill it. But if the book was passed you would be allocated a new one, and this was a great thrill! Newspapers and comics had fewer and poorer quality pages, and books to read were very hard to get.

Every year in September Mummy went into Liverpool. She walked up towards Dale Street where there was a printing shop. It didn't look like a bookshop, but we knew that it could get hold of annuals for Christmas. Mummy ordered several, knowing that if we were lucky we might be able to get about half that number. As December approached we looked out for the postcard arriving from the printing shop. As soon as it did, Mummy dropped everything and went into Liverpool, coming back with her precious parcel. We had to wait until Christmas day to see which ones she had been able to get. I did hope I might have both "School Friend" and "Girls' Crystal".

Occasionally a whisper would reach us on the "grapevine". One of the toyshops in town had had a consignment of dinky toys. We dropped everything. We couldn't get there quickly enough. Already there would be a long, long queue. If we were lucky we would reach the counter before all the cars were sold, and would be allowed to buy just one. You couldn't choose which one. But we were delighted with whatever we had been allocated. John would be able to have at least one new toy at Christmas. One Christmas, when John was about three, Mr Foggett, who was good at woodwork, made him a toy fort. Mummy was horrified at the price he charged for it. But she didn't have any option. She paid up, and was grateful. Father Christmas was having a bad time! John's expectations were never excessive, and his requests were sometimes quite original. One year he asked Father Christmas to bring him 'Three pots of jam and three pieces of toast!' And, brought up on wartime rations, he seemed to prefer simple food. When offered the tempting treat of ice cream, he would turn it down in favour of his favourite rice pudding.

Sometimes, as a present, we were given a drawing pad. These measured about six inches by eight, and the paper was pure white, and quite thick, a real luxury during the war. Thrilled with my present, I allocated these precious sheets of paper to my best work. Deciding what to draw was an exciting exercise which required much careful thought. The secret was to make the pad last as long as possible.

Nana brought home "stamp edging" from her office, together with used envelopes. The edges from a sheet of postage stamps , when licked, served as a useful predecessor to sellotape. The envelopes were used with gummed labels to cover the original address. We wrote to Daddy every week. Mummy wrote twice a week. I enjoyed writing letters, telling him our latest news. He wrote to us, too, separate letters for each of us. He didn't give us much news, but commented on each item of the news which we had given him in our letters. And I liked the familiar ending - 'Ever your loving Daddy.'

We were on the trolley bus going into town. Mummy was carrying her letter to Daddy. We would post it in town. I glanced at the envelope. 'Mummy!' I gasped, 'You've put Second Lieutenant!' Mummy was horrified, but was glad that I had noticed. Daddy was a Captain now, but Mummy was so used to writing "2nd Lieut." that she had done it without thinking. We got off the bus at the next stop and went back home. We put the letter in a new envelope, addressed it again, and went back to town.

One Easter-time Daddy was on a Training Course in North Wales, and we stayed in a boarding house in Rhyl for a few days so that we would be able to see him during his "off duty" periods. These times proved to be longer than expected, as an accident resulting in a broken thumb prevented him from taking part in motor bike instruction.

We had one bedroom in the boarding house, with two beds. Mummy and Helen were to have one bed, and John and I would sleep in the other. But we were so cold that we all squeezed into the one bed for warmth! Not only were we very cold, but we were also very hungry. We walked along the cold, dreary Promenade in search of food. To our delight, we found a small cafe which served delicious plums and custard. Each day, as soon as we had finished our mid-day meal, we walked along the Promenade for our daily treat: mouth-watering juicy yellow plums and even yellower custard. I wonder where those plums came from? Plums at Easter-time were an unusual luxury.

I also wonder how I had managed to take with me on that holiday a small bag of cream filled chocolates, which I had hidden among my clothes. Four of these were carefully wrapped in scraps of paper, and I proudly distributed them to the family with my greetings on Easter Sunday morning.

Appeals for the war effort were broadcast regularly on the wireless. Scrap metal was needed, as it could be recycled into battleships and aeroplanes. All the railings and metal gates were taken away. Our fence was made of wood, and so was our gate, so we didn't lose them. But the railings and gates disappeared from school, and those at the cemetery went, too. Some patriotic people even parted with their surplus saucepans!

"Waste not, want not" was a familiar wartime slogan. Soap was another precious commodity. It was a crime to drop it into the bath water. And the water itself had to be saved. Many people had a line drawn round their bath at the recommended 5 inch water level. Helen and I always shared the same water. When the tablet of soap became too small to be used in the bathroom it was deposited in a small wire-mesh container with a wire handle. With several scraps of soap inside, you could swish this around in the washing up water, to make it more efficient for removing grease from dishes.

Often we were encouraged in our efforts by the commanding and reassuring voice of our wartime hero, Mr Winston Churchill. When we heard his voice on the wireless we always stopped what we were doing and listened. He inspired patriotism. He gave us hope. No matter how depressing the news, he spurred us on to further effort.

Every evening, before the nine o clock news, I listened to my favourite programme. I would be all ready for bed, but begged not to go through to my bedroom in the shelter until I had heard all the National Anthems. It was stirring music. The National Anthem of each of the allied countries was played in full. I knew them all, and could identify each country by the first few notes of its anthem. Listening to this programme made me feel very proud of "our side."

Then I went to bed and prayed for the war to be over, for Daddy to come home, and for our side to win. But I felt sorry for God. He had a big problem. I was sure that there would be children whose countries were on the "other side" who were praying the same prayer. How could the God of the whole world decide whose prayers to answer? He couldn't please everybody, could he? How was he to decide which side would win?

Prep. R, Lower 1 and Brownies

The bath water was becoming more and more salty. 'Six sevens are forty two, seven sevens are forty nine, eight sevens are . . . ' I sobbed. Mummy was trying to help, and was insisting that I had to remember the whole table up to twelve sevens before I got out of the bath. Miss Headridge had said that I would have to "stay down" if I didn't know my tables. I wouldn't be able to go up to Prep. R in September. Rote learning was always a problem for me. It still is. I had no problem whatever with multiplication sums, or any other kind of sums, for that matter. I always got my sums right. But I couldn't recite the lists of tables which other children seemed to find easy to learn. Did I manage to deceive Miss Headridge? Or did she relent? I certainly hadn't managed to commit these wretched tables to memory by the end of the school year, but I went into Prep. R with the rest of the Form in September.

There was one more disagreement which I had with Miss Headridge before I left Prep. A. The fabric with which we were making our knitting aprons was harsh, and it was a muddy brown colour. With our compasses we had drawn circles and segments of circles on the large pocket, which we were to outline with backstitch in coloured wool. Then we were to edge the whole garment with blanket stitch. We could choose two contrasting colours. In an effort to brighten up the dull fabric, I had my eye on a bright red and a bright yellow. First I stitched round the edge of the large circle with red, then I started to outline the segments in yellow. I was quite pleased with the effect. But Miss Headridge was not pleased. Red and yellow, she said, did not go well together. She tried to persuade me that brown would look better than yellow with the red. Perhaps it would, to her eyes, but not to mine. However, grown-ups always know best. When I took the knitting apron home at the end of the term, I was very disappointed with it. I was still convinced that a bright splash of yellow would have improved it! But by the end of the Summer holiday all differences of opinion with Miss Headridge were forgotten with the excitement of going back into Prep. R.

Prep. R's Formroom was downstairs, and opened onto the Hall. I remember very little about it. I have even forgotten the name of the Form mistress. But I do recall one very embarrassing incident. At "recess" time we would all troop into the room next door, where the crates of milk and boxes of straws were waiting.

As we finished our milk we went out to play. I hovered at the door: a vital decision had to be made. I was dying to go to the lavatory. Should I ask to go there first, and then come back to drink my milk? The others might have all gone out by the time I got back, and I didn't want to miss my milk. Could I wait until I had drunk my milk, then dash to the lavatory on the way out? I made the wrong decision. I was halfway through my third of a pint of milk when, with horror, I felt the stream of water running down my legs. Soon there was a puddle on the floor. Quickly I poured the rest of my milk onto the puddle, and announced that I had spilled my milk. But I didn't deceive anyone. I was sent to the cookery kitchen to request the loan of a spare pair of knickers.

There may have been little of note happening in Prep. R, but Lower I was certainly a memorable form. Our Form mistress was Miss Neville Martin. She always had her full title, to distinguish her from the other Miss Martin, who was, I think, the School Secretary. Miss Neville Martin kept us on our toes. She was jolly, and liked to share a joke with us. How fortunate that we had arrived in her Form just as we had reached the age to appreciate her kind of joke! There was a lot of laughter in Miss Neville Martin's form. And I was especially favoured, as I was her "little backstitcher."

I won this accolade for the way in which I attached the bias binding to the edge of my blue cotton apron. These aprons were not a bit like our knitting aprons. The material was fine cotton, and we were using small needles and fine thread to stitch on the bright blue binding. When Miss Neville Martin requested that the back stitches be as small as possible I owed that mine would be smaller than anyone else's. And they were. From that moment I became Miss Neville Martin's "little backstitcher." By the time we came to hem down the second side of the binding - a very wearysome business - I had convinced myself that I was a good stitcher. How wrong I was! But how clever Miss Neville Martin was to inspire me in this fashion!

Miss Neville Martin wrote with a most beautiful neat, even script which everyone admired and tried to emulate. And again, I tried harder than anybody. Miss Neville Martin explained patiently how and why her script was economical of time, ink and effort. There were no unnecessary loops and twirls. The ascenders and descenders each had their own particular heights. The "t's" and "b's" were shorter than "h's" and "l's". We practised and practised. We compared our efforts, and strove to improve. Praise from Miss Neville Martin was a sufficient reward. If the inkwells became blocked with dust and bits of blotting paper we washed them out, and refilled them from the enamel can with the long, thin spout which was kept in the cupboard. If a pen nib became "crossed" (this was your own fault, it was caused through holding the pen holder at the wrong angle) Miss Neville Martin could always find a new one. Each week we would be supplied with a new sheet of blotting paper. Poor equipment would not be allowed to impede our progress in calligraphy. I don't know how Miss Neville Martin acquired her seemingly endless supplies of equipment, because in Miss Headridge's form we had always been short of these commodities.

It was Miss Neville Martin who initiated us into the mysteries of the magic lantern, which we were told was an "epidiascope." Miss Neville Martin was not afraid of teaching us how to use technical language. She took us over into the Lecture Theatre in North Block, and we perched on the tiered seating. Then she turned out the lights and projected some holiday postcards onto the screen. We were intrigued.

One day Mrs Varley came into our Formroom to talk to Miss Neville Martin. Mrs Varley was not a Prep School mistress. She taught English to the Senior Girls over in North Block. She was one of the very few married ladies on the Staff. Only since the war had married women joined the Cowley Staff. It was not so very many years since anyone choosing to marry would immediately lose their teaching job. The big girls, Mrs Varley told us, were preparing to give a performance of "A Midsummer Night's

Dream" in her garden at Haresfinch. She was looking for four smaller girls to play the part of the four fairies: Pease-blossom, Cobweb, Moth and Mustard-seed. Miss Neville Martin chose her little "backstitcher" as one of the fairies!

We wouldn't need much practice, Mrs Varley said, because the parts were very small. She would tell us nearer the time when we were to go for a rehearsal. Our frilly net dresses were all in pastel shades, Pease-blossom had pink, Cobweb had pale blue, Moth had pale green, and mine, because I was Mustard-seed, was yellow.

The great day arrived, and we were to go to Haresfinch for the rehearsal. The big girls would be riding there on their bikes, and four of them had offered to transport the fairies. As instructed, we waited by the bicycle sheds. I was lifted onto a saddle, and the owner of the bike had to ride standing up all the way. It was a very wobbly ride, and it was difficult to know where to put my feet. I clung tightly to the waist of my chauffeur. Mrs Varley's garden was in Green Leach Lane. It was huge. I think it's some sort of public garden now. The fairies, as instructed, took up their position behind a bush at the edge of the large lawn. We weren't needed till Act III. It seemed a very long time before our names were called by Titania, and we emerged to say our few words. Mrs Varley made us say them over and over again, because we weren't speaking loudly enough. It was quite difficult to shout "And I" in a loud voice. After we had made our short appearance we were taken into Mrs Varley's big house and given a drink while we waited for our bicycle ride back to school. The rest of Lower I must have been very envious! We were so proud to have been chosen as Titania's four fairies.

On one afternoon each week Miss Neville Martin read to us from "The Secret Garden". It was an opportunity to relax. Miss Neville Martin's voice was soothing, and my mind switched easily into its daydreaming mode. I thought about how happy I was. I thought about how lucky I was. I wondered why the wind was whistling so loudly. It was something to do with the gaps in the window frames. It didn't matter if it was pouring with rain outside. We were warm and dry. We were comfortable. When, two or three years later, I read "The Secret Garden" for myself I was surprised to find it a fresh, new story. I hadn't heard it before. I had daydreamed away the whole of the time that Miss Neville Martin had been reading to us. I hadn't listened to one word of the story.

I was a very poor listener, and preferred to read to myself rather than to listen to someone else reading. I still do. Suitable books at home were limited. Apart from my beloved Christmas annuals, the ones I had been given as presents included The Water Babies, Aesop's Fables, Grimm's Fairy Tales, Hans Anderson's Fairy Tales, Through the Looking Glass, The Complete Works of Shakespeare and The Holy Bible. The inscription on the flyleaf of the Shakespeare indicates that this was given to me at Christmas, 1936, when I was just five years old! The Hans Anderson was a sixth birthday present. I think that probably very few books specifically for children were published during the war. But I still had my Winnie-the-Pooh books, and Mummy's "Katy" books and her "Pollyanna" books. I was very fond of Pollyanna, and was most impressed by her "glad" game. If anyone was unhappy, all they had to do was to think of something to be glad about. Pollyanna could always think of something. She was right - I tried it, and it worked!

Nana liked reading, too, and she borrowed books from Boots Subscription Library in town. Once when Daddy was home on leave he took me into town and paid my subscription so that I could join the children's section of Boots Library. It was the best present he could possibly have bought me. Each of the books had a little green shield stuck to the front cover with "Boots" inscribed on it. Each book had a tiny metal ring attached to the top of the spine. The lady behind the desk took your chosen book and slotted the tiny metal tag which was attached to your ticket with a green string through the metal ring in your book. Then you could take it home. Choosing was difficult at first, but I soon learned to find the type of book that I enjoyed. An adventure story by Enid Blyton or Arthur Ransome was a great find. Then there were stories about twins living in different countries of the world. But after a while I became hooked on school stories. "The Chalet School" was my favourite, but anything by Angela Brazil was certain to be a good read. Those schoolgirl heroines provided an ideal role model. They never boasted, always owned up, never told lies, never let down a friend - what a lot to live up to! I enjoyed sad stories as well as happy ones, and wept copiously over "The Land of Far Beyond" and "A Peep Behind the Scenes." I was a member of that Library till it closed and, by then, I don't think there were many books in the children's section which I hadn't read.

When I was engrossed in a library book it must have been difficult for anyone to prise me away from it. But I never wanted to read on Brownie nights. Anne and I were eight when we joined the Brownies. Auntie Jessie had a friend who lived in Kiln Lane whose daughter belonged to the 2nd Eccleston Pack. So Anne and I went there, too. We met in the Congregational Church at the bottom of Kiln Lane. Now it is a Church Hall because a new Church has been built. In 1940 the building served both as a Church and a meeting Hall. Anne and I were a bit apprehensive as we walked down Kiln Lane and called, as arranged, at the house of Auntie Jessie's friend. We were taken to the Church, and introduced to Brown Owl. As soon as we joined in that big circle and skipped round, holding hands and singing 'We're the Brownies, here's our aim, lend a hand and play the game' I knew I was going to enjoy Brownies. I was in the "Little People" Six, and had to learn their song, too. When it was our turn we skipped around the toadstool and sang 'We though known as little people, aim as high as any steeple.' The words didn't make much sense, but it was a good tune with a strong skipping rhythm.

It seemed a long time before Anne and I had earned the privilege of becoming fully fledged Brownies, and were able to wear our brown cotton dresses with their leather belts, and matching hats with turned up brims and elastic to go under the chin. We had, at last, mastered the art of folding the cumbersome yellow triangle into what passed for a tie, though the loop that, in school ties went round your neck, in Brownie ties hung down to your belt. The ends that, in school ties, hung down the front, in

In uniform at last; At the back, Anne Hart and Barbara
Murray. In front: Barbara and Helen.

107

Brownie ties had to be tied in a reef knot under your collar. That meant you had to learn to tie a reef knot behind your back or - more accurately - behind your neck! I nearly burst out of my tie with pride when finally the shiny badge was pinned on it, after I had solemnly promised to be a good Brownie.

We had a busy time in Brownies. We skipped and we played with balls. We tied up parcels and we polished shoes. We folded clothes, made beds and washed dishes. We had treasure hunts and picnics. In the Summer we trailed along the footpath beside the brook in Watery Lane to play on the stepping stones. We took off our shoes and socks and paddled.

Brown Owl, was a hard taskmaster. She would not pass any shoddy work. The instep of the shoe must be polished with as much care as the upper. I had spent many weary hours on my "darn." The threads were evenly spaced, and I had carefully woven over and under each one. Pleased with the result, I held up my darned sock for inspection. But it wouldn't pass. I had failed to allow for shrinkage. I should have left small loops of wool at the end of each row. The darning wool was new, and would shrink in the wash. The sock was old, and would not shrink in the wash. In despair I retreated to my Six corner, and patiently began to unpick all my careful work.

On the second Sunday in each month we went to the Congregational Church for Church Parade. We gathered with the Guides in the little cloakroom by the door, then filed into our reserved seats at the front of the Church. During the first hymn three Guides walked down the aisle, the middle one carrying a huge Union Jack. I wondered whether I would ever fulfil my great ambition to carry that flag myself one day? Happily, I did, many, many times, and never lost my sense of pride in being chosen for that solemn duty.

For a short time Helen and I went to Sunday School at Eccleston Congregational Church on Sunday afternoons. Brown Owl was one of the Sunday School teachers. She told us Bible stories, and we were rewarded for listening with small "stickers" depicting Biblical scenes and texts. We wore our best hats and coats for Sunday School, and our best shoes, too. Helen was sometimes a nuisance when we were walking back up Kiln Lane, especially when Edward Jones was with us. They always wanted to stop and play by the brook. One day Helen and Edward paddled in their best shoes! When we got home I found that I was in as much trouble as they were. I should have been able to stop them.

Trying to make sense
of a confusing world

'But you'll have to put her on the fire' Nana said, in my dream. Mummy didn't want to burn me up completely, but if my finger got burnt I would have to sit in the fire till I had burned away altogether. It would make Mummy very sad, but she would have to do what Nana said. This was a recurring dream. Fortunately I always woke up just as I was about to be placed in the centre of a fiercely burning fire. The fire was the one in the middle room at 22, Hard Lane. Was this dream, I wonder, triggered by some over-zealous warning about the danger of fire?

Helen has reminded me of a real-life episode relating to this dream. She remembers me being extremely upset at the time, yet I seem to have blotted the whole episode from my own memory. Lily, the elderly maid we had at Cranley when John was a baby, was in charge. Mummy had gone to town. We were in the lounge and John was in his playpen. I think that Helen and I must have been quarrelling over a rag doll dressed in a blue velvet sailor suit. Lily couldn't cope. She took the doll and threw it onto the fire. When Mummy came in I apparently insisted that she rake through the ashes to rescue the remains of the poor, burnt creature. This was the end of Lily's reign. In the belief that a younger person might have more patience with children, Irene was appointed.

For years I clung to the notion that my dolls had feelings. My common sense told me otherwise, yet my emotions wouldn't listen to my common sense. Once, when I was still in Miss Fitch's Form I left behind at school a teddy bear dressed in checked pyjamas. It was Friday, and I was frantic throughout the whole weekend, till we were able to go back to school to rescue him. In my troubled sleep the pattern on his pyjamas became a nightmare. I grasped at it, but couldn't reach it. In desperation I hid from it, but could see it even with my eyes shut. Long after we had retrieved the missing teddy I would recoil in horror every time I saw a pattern or design similar to that on teddy's pyjamas. Sometimes I saw this pattern slowly develop in the embers of the fire, and would have to avert my gaze.

Another common childhood dream was more prevalent after we moved to Cranley. But it was a dream about 22, Hard Lane. I was walking home, and would turn into Hard Lane from Greenfield Road. The row of houses opposite the Abbey Hotel had changed. My house wasn't there any more. Home and family had disappeared, and I was completely alone in the world. Frantically I began to search for familiar landmarks - anything which might show me that the world which I recognised still existed.

The dream-world was always puzzling and disturbing. Nothing was ever quite right. And sometimes the real world was not quite right, either. Often, as a child, I had a strange ability to know what was going to happen before it happened. Sometimes, before arriving at a new place, a picture of it would flash into my mind, and I had the strange feeling that I had been there before, though I knew that this wasn't the case. I wished that I could be wrong, but I was never wrong. I was always right in every tiny detail, and I didn't like it. Sometimes I would know what someone was going to say before they said it. Then I waited, with baited breath, hoping that my premonition wouldn't be right. But it always was right. I did so want the world to behave in a logical, consistent way which I was able to understand. But it didn't.

Always I strove to anchor down my little world, by coming to grips with the relationship between places, by understanding the route to follow from one place to another. I think I "drew" maps in my mind. We were travelling towards Southport, so I expect it was Saturday afternoon. We were in the car, so it must have been before the war. Occupied with my own thoughts, I started to think about "places." The place we had come from was St Helens. The place we were going to was Southport. The place we were passing through was Rainford. But what of the bits in between? Sometimes there was a farm in the middle of somewhere which didn't seem to be a "place" at all. Where were you if you were in a gap between places? How could I find out?

I waited till the last houses in Rainford were behind us and then asked 'Where are we now?' 'Rainford' I was told. I had asked too soon. I waited till we were much further on, and there was nothing to see but fields on each side of the road. 'Where are we now?' I asked. 'I've just told you' came the reply with a hint of impatience behind it, 'We're in Rainford.' Dare I try again further on? By this time my problem was really gnawing away at my mind, and I was desperate for a solution. So I risked it. 'Where are we now?' I asked. But adult patience had its limits. 'If you ask that question again' I was told firmly, 'You can get out of the car and walk the rest of the way.'

It was many years before I saw and understood a map of the local area. Why was it that, at school, we had maps of the world, and maps of Great Britain, which had very little meaning at the time? I would have been fascinated to have seen a map of St Helens, and it would have helped to straighten out some of my muddled thinking about "places." The war didn't help, because all the place names had been removed from the signposts, so as to confuse the enemy if they were to invade.

When I walked to and from school on my own, I took a variety of different routes, and gradually learned the network of roads running between Gamble Avenue and Windleshaw Road. Then I started to wonder which was the shortest route, and took to counting my footsteps in an attempt to estimate the length of various journeys. It was fun, and served to pass the time if I had chosen a particularly boring route, such as walking the full length of Windleshaw Road.

We were at Anne's house and Margaret was ill in bed. The bed was downstairs in the middle room. Anne's family was sleeping downstairs now, because of the air raids. Anne and I were sitting beside the bed to keep Margaret company. We were all sewing, but I can't remember what we were making. I have a feeling we may have been dressing tiny dolls. We were short of a small item which could only be purchased in town. We couldn't finish whatever it was we were making without it. We decided that Anne should go to town, and Margaret and I would continue with the sewing. Margaret devised a game to pass the time while Anne was away. We would talk through Anne's trip to town, 'She is walking down Hard Lane ... Now she has met Grandma Murray, and has stopped to chat ... Now she is waiting for the bus ... Now the bus has arrived and the people are getting off ... Now the conductor has his pole and is changing over the trolleys to the other track ... Now Anne is getting on the bus . . .' We continued with this game, allowing what we thought were suitable intervals between each of our statements, 'Now she is getting off the bus ... Now she is crossing Greenfield Road ... Now she is walking up Hard Lane ... Now she is turning in at the gate.' I looked through the window in great excitement, and there she was! We were right!

One day Miss Neville Martin was talking to us about time and motion studies. What a fascinating idea! Many dreary routine tasks could be made much more interesting if you were working out the quickest and easiest way of tackling them. It was an entertaining game, and I played it often.

Having been asked to lay the table for tea, I worked out my strategy. The table was covered with books and papers. If I stood at one end, cleared the books as far as I could reach, spread the cloth as far as I could reach, then laid the knives and forks at that end before walking round to the other end and repeating the process, this would be saving of time and energy. I was happily playing my game, and was just completing the first end of the table when Mummy came in. She was not pleased. I suppose it did look a bit odd. One end of the table was laid for tea, and the other end was still covered with books and papers. If that was the way I chose to lay the table, I needn't bother. Mummy would lay the table herself, and I could go straight upstairs to bed. After that episode I only played my "time and motion" game when I was sure that no-one was watching.

Why was I so poor at explaining my problems to Mummy? I suspect that much of what appears to adults as "naughty" behaviour in the young is the result of a misunderstanding. I know this frequently happened to me. Yet adults often have a very difficult time trying to answer children's questions. I expect my question about how far you would have to travel in a straight line before you fell off the end of the earth is quite a common one. Yet the answer, that you can continue until you are back where you started, was quite incomprehensible to me at the time I asked the question.

It was Mummy's answer to one difficult question which made me realise, with shock and horror, that even grown-ups don't have all the right answers. Some of the information which I was being fed at school didn't stand up to my fast growing powers of reasoning. The theory that humans were descended from apes was surely in conflict with the theory that we are all descended from Adam and Eve. Could Mummy sort this one out for me? 'I expect animals were developing into people in one part of the world' she suggested, 'While Adam and Eve lived in another part of the world.' Not only was this a totally unsatisfactory answer, but I realised that Mummy didn't have an answer at all, and had only made this one up to stop me from asking any further questions on the subject.

There were three worlds which I had to sort out. First there was the dream world. How did you know when you were dreaming and when you were awake? Supposing the dream-world was real, and the real world was only a dream? When you thought you were dreaming, could you check that it was really only a dream? One way I had heard of was to pinch yourself. So I decided to try this. One night when I was dreaming I pinched my arm, and immediately woke up. My arm was hurting, so I deduced that this was quite a useful way of checking whether or not you were dreaming. What we thought we knew as the real world raised questions, too. Anne and I often discussed them. When we both saw something which we agreed was green, for example, were we seeing the same colour? Was my green Anne's blue, or my red her yellow? Did Anne really exist, or was she merely a figment of my imagination? Was there a "real" world which she and I shared?

And, finally, there was the "after death" world, the one we called "heaven". How far did you have to travel up into the sky before you got there? And heaven must be very crowded, if all those who had ever lived were up there. Would there be room for us when it was time for us to go? Could the people up there see us down here? And the biggest question of all was 'How do you get there?' Why do we put dead bodies down into the ground in order for them to fly up into the sky?

A "full-size" bike, and other eleven-year-old pleasures

'I don't want you to tell me what it is,' I lied to Helen, because I knew she had been sworn to secrecy. But I suspected that, now that my legs were long enough, I might be lucky enough to get a full-size bike for my eleventh birthday. There was a way I could confirm my suspicions without Helen revealing her secret. 'Just tell me' I begged. 'When I get my present, will you be getting something new, too?' 'Yes!' she beamed, believing her secret to be still intact. So I was right. I would have my full-size bike, Helen would have my fairy cycle and John could use the tricycle.

That I had guessed the secret didn't in any way lessen my delight when I ran downstairs on the morning of my birthday and found the bike in the hall. Of course I had known that it couldn't have been a new bike because, along with so many other things, new bicycles were unobtainable during the war. But Mr Cook was good at renovating second-hand bikes, and this one certainly looked as good as new. I could hardly wait to get dressed. Having ridden round the house a couple of times, I rode straight down the road to show my exciting present to Dadda Toddy.

It was a pity that I wouldn't be able to go to school on my bike yet. Bikes weren't allowed at school until you were in the Second Form. It was a rule. You could go to school on a bike in the Second Form, you could use a fountain pen in the Third Form, and you could wear a wrist watch in the Fifth Form. I was only in the First Form, so I had plenty of treats to look forward to.

Miss Neville Martin had prepared us well to take that giant step from the Prep. School into the Senior School. It was very exciting. She explained that she was going to divide the register into four equal parts, and each quarter of the Form would move into one of the four First Forms. Because the initial letter of my surname was "M" I would be going into 1c. I was glad that Barbara Murray was in the same quarter as me. There would be six of us from Lower 1 in 1c, and the rest of the form would be made up of "scholarship" children from Elementary Schools. I wished my surname had begun with an A or a B. It would have been nice to boast about being in 1a. It sounded far superior to 1c.

As it happened, I was lucky to be going to 1c, because my Form Mistress was to be Miss Wood. Miss Wood was young, and kind, and very helpful. It was a surprise to discover that she would only be teaching us when we were learning French, and that we would need to get to know a wide range of different Mistresses. Our Form room was still in South Block, and opened into the Hall, but this was only a base from which we loaded our satchels and travelled to all the far corners of both North and South Blocks for our various lessons. What an interesting time we were going to have, and how well Miss Neville Martin had prepared us to enjoy our new challenge!

We had, of course, peeped into the science lab, through the glass panel in the door as we walked past on the balcony of South Block, but now we actually went inside, and perched on the high stools to reach the well-worn benches with their built-in sinks and the gas outlets for connecting up the bunsen burners. There was a huge chart on the wall listing all the chemical symbols, and through the glass-fronted cupboards we could see an intriguing array of strange-shaped bottles containing liquids and crystals of every hue. I couldn't wait to get started!

We went across to North Block and climbed two flights of stairs to the very top of the building, and fòund the Art Studio. Here we met Miss "Art" Duncan. Her middle name had been added to distinguish her from another Miss Duncan on the Staff. Miss Art Duncan was quite a character. She was small and plump, with a mass of untidy white hair which she tried, unsuccessfully, to keep in check with numerous hairpins. She was hopeless at keeping order, and we shamelessly took advantage of this. We chatted constantly when we should have been getting on with our work. Miss Art Duncan muttered, over and over again. 'Somebody's inclined to talk, somebody's inclined to talk,' nodding her head and scattering hairpins as she repeated her favourite refrain. We totally ignored her complaint.

Miss Art Duncan was a particular embarrassment to me because she chose me as her "favourite." I did not gain this position because of anything I had done to deserve it. I think the only reason was because she had taught Mummy when she had been at Cowley, and Mummy had been very good at art. I must have been a great disappointment. I was hopeless at art, and didn't appreciate it when my inadequate efforts received greater praise than they deserved.

It was in 1c that I first met Miss Clarke and Miss Willis, and I have clear memories of both these good ladies. They were outstandingly able teachers, and I have cause to be grateful to them for my love of history and of mathematics. Miss Clarke taught history, and it was clear that Miss Clarke knew and loved her history. She knew how to make history come alive. If she had not been a teacher, Miss Clarke would have been a good actress. As she moved around the front of the room (I don't ever remember Miss Clarke sitting down) she became Sir Walter Raleigh or Elizabeth the First. She became Sir Francis Drake, a Spanish galleon - even a whole armada! Her voice changed as she took the role of each character. She waved her arms around, and she leapt from the floor. She became excited in the heat of battle, and you could almost see the imaginary sword in her hand. She became dismayed as she collapsed across the desk, injured and defeated. We loved it all, and we remembered it.

Miss Willis was another who loved her subject. She loved mathematics, and I did, too. She loved a complex problem which could be worked through in logical stages until it reached a neat and satisfying conclusion. I did, too. I loved those trains which left different stations at different times, and travelled towards each other at different speeds. I loved those baths which filled from taps which allowed a particular amount of water to enter in a particular number of seconds. I loved those rolls of wallpaper which could be cut to fit rooms of various dimensions. One day Miss Willis announced that we would play some number games, and we were to choose a number between one and twenty. Then she asked us to apply all manner of calculations to our chosen number: we were to divide, to multiply, to add, to subtract, and then when we told her the result of all our calculations she told us our original number. She was right! We were intrigued. We tried again using different numbers, different calculations. Every time she was right. We begged her to tell us how it was done. 'In the next lesson,' she said, and left us guessing. There are probably those who find it difficult to imagine that a Form of eleven year olds could be looking forward to a maths lesson with such eager anticipation. But these people

Cowley Girls' School, St. Helens: a Form Room

Cowley Girls' School, St Helens: The School Hall

Cowley Girls' School, St. Helens: The Chemical Laboratory

Cowley Girls' School, St. Helens: The Art Room

Cowley Girls' School, St. Helens: The Playing Field

Cowley Girls' School, St. Helens: The Gymnasium (c.1951)

were not fortunate enough to be taught by Miss Willis. Miss Willis finally shared her secret. Every time we thought of a number, she thought of x. Every time we applied an arithmetical process to our number, she did the same with her x. And then she showed us how to find the number which x represented. We were surprised when Miss Willis told us we had been doing algebra. We thought we had been playing number games.

Now that we were in the First Form we were introduced to other games, too. We were divided into teams, given our coloured bands, and taken outside to be initiated into the game of netball. We practised throwing, catching, dodging, marking and shooting. We were taken to the gym. We took off our gym slips and our ties, and, in our navy blue knickers and our green blouses we were introduced to wall bars, ropes, vaulting horses and benches. I loved it all, and felt sorry for those who were not lucky enough to go to a school like Cowley.

We went across to the hall in North Block for music. I was quite prepared to enjoy this lesson, too. I had always liked to sing and dance and listen to music. But it was here that I was to descend with a nasty bump from my cheerful, elated state. Pride does come before a fall, and I had been proud of all the exciting new things I was entitled to do now that I had climbed to First Form status. Our music Mistress was rather a stern lady with iron grey hair swept back into a severe bun. The first thing she must do, she told us, was to find out who could sing and who couldn't. Each in our turn, in alphabetical order, we were to climb onto the stage, alone, and sing. I was terrified. It was a long time before the "M's" were reached, and by this time my voice had almost disappeared altogether with fright. All the other Mistresses we had met had been smilingly encouraging and reassuring when we had first met them. Not so this lady whose name I have forgotten. I think our ability to sing was graded from 1 to 6. Or it may have been from A to F. I don't know whether my efforts earned a 6 or an F. It was one or the other. I was devastated. My form mates were sympathetic. Those of us deemed unable to sing in tune were advised to mouth the words when the others sang in unison. Some of the songs which we learned had lovely haunting melodies. My favourites were "David of the White Rock" and "Danny Boy". I would have liked to have raised my voice in unison with the rest of the Form. But I daren't. I might have spoiled it. It never occurred to me at the time that this music Mistress might have been appointed to teach girls with voices like mine how to sing in tune. It obviously didn't occur to her, either.

At the end of the first week we came back to Miss Wood for "Form period". By this time our desks were full of new exercise books, each one labelled with one of the new subjects to which we had been introduced during the week. And we had collected text books to match each of these. We were to take all the books home with us, cover them with brown paper, and write our name, Form, and subject on the front of each one. One subject to which I had been looking forward was missing. Cookery classes had been suspended for the duration of the war. Now that all the ingredients were rationed none could be spared for us to practise our culinary skills. Again I was fortunate. I was encouraged to learn to cook at home.

Miss Wood had one final piece of interesting information for us. This was the news we had been waiting for all the week. She would tell us which "House" we were to join. The Cowley "Houses" were named after Saints, and I was to be in St Helena's. Our colour was orange, and those to be in our House were given their little strips of orange corded ribbon to sew onto their gym slips. With these precious bits of ribbon in our pockets we were dispatched to North Block to find our Head of House. She was a prefect. As well as her orange ribbon, she had both a prefect's badge and a deportment badge on her gym slip. We listened intently as she told us that "order" marks and "commendations" were both to be reported to her, as they would be recorded and used either to degrade or enhance the reputation of our House. We vowed to support our House through thick and thin, and were totally convinced that St Helena's was the best House in the School.

By the end of the year I was to have my name called out at Prayer time and walk proudly up onto the platform in South Block Hall, where Miss Hurt would present me with a deportment badge. Mummy would sew the small green shield with its "C" for Cowley beside the orange ribbon.

Now that I was eleven it was decided that it was time for me to learn how to swim. Anne had lessons from Mrs Birch at the Boundary Road baths but Nana had been very nervous about my going in the water because of my ears. I was nervous, too. I wasn't sure that my confidence would be sufficient to allow me to take my feet off the bottom of the bath. There were two baths at Boundary Road. The smaller one was for ladies only. The larger one was sometimes for men only, and sometimes for "mixed bathing." Mrs Birch gave lessons in the smaller pool. After a few basic directions, Mrs Birch told me to put the ring at the end of her rope around my waist. Then she towed me back and forth across the pool. After a while she appeared to lose interest in me, and turned to have a chat with

Mummy on the side of the pool. At that moment I lost my footing and disappeared under the water. Fortunately Mummy noticed, and pointed out my plight. I was rescued, spluttering, and gasping for breath. After several sessions with Mrs Birch I realised that I was making little progress, and decided that the time had come for me to teach myself to swim.

I acquired an inflatable rubber ring, and practised swimming back and forth with it fully inflated. Then I let out a little air, and practised again. Each time I went to the baths I let out a bit more air. Finally I was swimming with a totally deflated ring, and decided that I might as well discard it altogether. The next time Daddy came home on leave I wanted to surprise him. So we chose a "mixed bathing" time and went into the larger pool. Daddy wouldn't have been allowed to watch me swimming in the "ladies only" pool. He sat in the spectator's gallery and watched me showing off my new skill. 'You looked just like a little fish,' he complimented me afterwards.

By this time I was not only a swimmer, but an avid knitter, too. Mostly I knitted dolls' clothes, and especially liked to dress a tiny teddy which belonged to John. Recently I had learned to crochet, and the first garment which I made for myself was a crocheted beret. It had taken a great deal of effort. As it was made from a variety of oddments of left-over wool it was very colourful. I was proud of my achievement. It seemed to fit me quite well and, as berets were fashionable at the time, I thought I looked quite smart in it. At about the same time, Mummy had sewn some attractive navy blue felt pixie hoods for Helen and me, and had appliqued brightly coloured flowers made from oddments of felt on them for decoration. Auntie Jessie had made similar ones for Anne and Margaret, too.

It was New Year's Day. Helen, John and I were going to walk down Eaton Road together to say 'Happy New Year' to Momma and Dadda Toddy. We all had on our navy blue gabardine raincoats, and I came downstairs in my newly crocheted beret. I wanted to show my work to Dadda Toddy. I thought he would be pleased to see it. Mummy had other ideas! 'Take that off' she said firmly. 'You and Helen must dress alike on New Year's Day.' So I had to wear my pixie hood, as Helen was wearing hers. Mummy obviously didn't like my beret. I took it upstairs and hid it at the bottom of a drawer in my bedroom. I never wore it again.

Another milestone which was reached at about this time was the diphtheria innoculation. A new vaccine had been discovered which, it was claimed, would eliminate this dreaded disease once and for all. A nationwide campaign was organised to immunise all schoolchildren. Three injections were necessary, and we were called to the school clinic in Victoria Square on three separate occasions. We stood in the queue with our sleeves rolled up. Afterwards our arms ached for a couple of days, and some children wore red armbands round their sleeves to warn people not to bump into their sore arm.

I had a sore place, but it wasn't on my arm. It was on my waist. I had had a pain in my right side for some time, and had wondered what was causing it. Now I found that there was an ugly red patch with little white spots stretching round to my tummy. I showed it to Mummy, but she wasn't impressed. However, when it was still there a week later, alternately itching and hurting, she decided that Dr Merrick should be asked to call and have a look at it. 'Shingles,' he said, without hesitation 'I've never seen it in anyone so young.' Now that my affliction had a name, it merited a few days off school. Nana had worried me. 'You'd better keep an eye on it' she said. 'If it continues right round to the other side it could be fatal!'

Miss Wood: my Form Mistress in
1c and again in 3b

Although Mummy dismissed his idea without a second thought, I did have a careful look now and again to make sure the rash hadn't reached my left side. One afternoon, when I was still away from school, we met Miss Wood on the bus. 'Have you been ill?' she asked. Feeling guilty that I was away from school and not at home in bed I hung my head and said sheepishly 'Yes.' Mummy was cross. 'She hasn't been ill at all' she told Miss Wood, 'She's had shingles, that's all.' I hadn't meant to deceive Miss Wood. I had mistakenly thought that shingles was an illness.

I wasn't ill, but Nana was. Mummy was very worried about her. I couldn't understand Nana's illness. Usually Nana liked to talk about her ailments, but now she didn't talk at all. She didn't seem to hear when you spoke to her. She was very, very quiet, and I didn't like it. She was tired, and had spent a short time in hospital for a rest. Although she had been off work for some months the phone calls from Bishops continued, so she had little respite from her business worries. Although she was now sixty seven years old, and it was acknowledged that she was suffering from a "nervous breakdown", no-one thought of suggesting that she retire from her demanding job. She worried about the war, too. The Second World War had now continued for almost the same length of time as the First World War, and, in 1943, there were still no signs of it ending.

Deaths in the family

Helen and I were in the bath when Nana came upstairs to tell us that Auntie Eva had died. It was February, 1942. We knew that Auntie Eva had been very ill. She had suffered from bronchiectasis all her life, and had not been expected to live to a great age. That she had survived to the age of forty four, it was presumed, was due to the care which had been taken of her health throughout her life. Daddy had been home on "compassionate leave" for several days, and he and Mummy had been at "Weem" all day. Now they would soon be home. 'They might be upset' I warned Helen. I wondered if they would cry. I hoped they wouldn't. I didn't know what it was going to be like, as this was the first experience I had had of a death in my immediate family. It was a surprise and a relief to find that, the next day, life was relatively normal. Daddy had to go back to "Weem" to help Grandma and Grandpa to organise a funeral. Mummy was quite cheerful, and we went to school. It is significant that my only concerns were that my own little world should not be disturbed. I think I gave very little thought to Grandma and Grandpa's distress.

If I was little affected by this, my first experience of a family death, the following year, 1943, was to bring a tragedy which would shatter my childish innocence and change for ever my relationship with my Mother. I suppose that Nana's death was probably the most significant event to take place in the whole of my childhood.

125

Grandma and Grandpa Menzies outside
their bungalow, "Weem".

My Father must have had several periods of compassionate leave in
1943. Grandpa Menzies was now seriously ill in hospital, and Nana was
still unable to work because of severe depression which her doctors
described as "nervous exhaustion."

Grandpa Menzies died in the Providence hospital in May, 1943, shortly
before his seventy third birthday. I had been to visit him, and I think he
was embarrassed that I was, for the first time, seeing him in bed. He was
a very private person and, lying there in his private room, seemed not to
know what to say to his eleven year old granddaughter. After Grandpa
died, we had to devote more attention to Grandma, who was now living
alone. As Mummy was needed to care for Nana, and Daddy had to return
to his battalion, I was delegated to make regular visits to "Weem."

It was decided that Grandma Menzies would teach me to play the piano.
I would cycle down to Eccleston on Sunday afternoons for my piano lesson,
then have tea with Grandma before cycling home again. We soon
established a routine, and my Sunday visits to "Weem" continued for the
next three years. Grandma's kitchen was warm and cosy. Her comfortable
rocking chair stood by the old kitchen range, where the large black kettle
would be singing on the hob. The table beneath the window would be
neatly laid for tea for two. Grandma was very precise, and her table had

an orderly pattern which I admired. Sometimes there would be a boiled egg for tea, and sometimes some brawn. I didn't like brawn very much, and hoped it would be an egg. That is, until Grandma found a source for duck eggs and, as these were larger and a more unusual delicacy, they were supposed to be a treat.

Unfortunately I didn't appreciate this particular treat. There was always a plate of very thinly cut bread and butter, home-made jam in a glass dish, tinned fruit or jelly, and a home-made sponge cake. I enjoyed being an "only one" at Grandma's tea table and she listened patiently to all my school news.

I would be sent to wash my hands before we went through to the drawing room for the piano lesson. The passage down to the bathroom in the bungalow was dark. The worst bit was passing the curtain which was drawn around the coat rack where all the outdoor clothes were hanging. My imagination conjured up all sorts of strange beings which might be about to spring out from behind this curtain. In the Winter it was freezing cold in the drawing room. Grandma explained that she could never light a fire in this room because the chimney smoked. The small single-bar electric fire was too far away from the piano stool to warm us as I worked my way through the lengthy series of scales and arpeggios which were an essential preliminary to playing tunes. Then we would do some "theory," and I would draw some notes in my exercise book. Generally I enjoyed my piano lessons, though I certainly didn't escape censure if Grandma thought that I had not done sufficient practice during the week. She thought that one hour each evening was reasonable, but I was quite sure she didn't understand how much homework I had to do. Sometimes Grandma played for me. I admired the way her broad, flat fingertips slid gently across the ivory keys. I wished my legs, like hers, had been long enough to reach the pedals.

In the Summer I would be very hot after my cycle ride to Eccleston. Perspiring profusely, I would be desperately thirsty, and long for a drink of water. But I would have to sit in Grandma's rocking chair and cool off, while listening to her tale of woe about someone she knew who had drunk cold water while very hot and had dropped down dead. Only when it was established that I was quite cool would I be allowed to have a drink, and then only a small one!

Sometimes there were jobs I could help Grandma with on Sundays. Occasionally we took a saucer of milk and a soft cloth into the drawing room, with which I was instructed to clean the piano keys. Sometimes there were clean sheets or tablecloths waiting to be folded, a task which required two pairs of hands. Sometimes there was wool to be wound, and my arms would be required to hold the skeins while Grandma wound the balls. In the Autumn we went out into the orchard to gather apples. Then we wrapped them in small squares of newspaper, and laid them on trays in an outhouse to preserve them. As a reward for my help, I would be given some apples to take home. They were delicious. No apples bought in the shops, either before or since, ever tasted like those apples straight from the trees in the orchard at "Weem."

After a time I begged Mummy to think of a way we could ask Grandma not to serve duck eggs at teatime, without upsetting her. I knew it would be difficult. Fortunately Mummy was able to come to my aid. I don't know what she said, but I hoped she had been tactful.

I had no idea how to be tactful myself. It was one of my big problems, and it worried me. I'm afraid I must often have appeared rude and arrogant. Frequently I would bitterly regret something I had said while trying, and failing, to sound knowledgeable and grown-up. One thoughtless comment of mine I have regretted all my life. I had certainly not intended to be unkind, but I knew as soon as the words had left my mouth that they had been hurtful. And the last person I wanted to hurt was Nana. She had just come home from hospital, and was lying on the chesterfield when I came in from school. Full of my news of the day, I bounced into the lounge. 'Aren't you going to say you're pleased she's home?' reprimanded Mummy. The excuse that sprang to my lips - 'I didn't even notice she was there' - was unforgiveable. When I saw Nana's face I wished I had been brave enough to apologise. I was very sorry, but too proud to say so.

After she came home from hospital Nana slept in the big double bed with Mummy. She was suffering from insomnia, so I don't think Mummy got much sleep, either. Nana had started to worry that her memory was failing, and was constantly writing herself little notes and reminders on bits of paper and in notebooks all over the house. She worried that, if Daddy didn't come home, she would no longer be able to work to support the family. What would happen to us all?

We had just broken up from school for the Summer holiday. On Sunday morning, July 25th, Mummy came into my bedroom. I had been sleeping in Nana's bed. 'Nana has been taken ill in the night' she said 'and has gone to hospital.' I looked at her and I knew that Nana was dead. 'I want you to take Helen and John down to Auntie Marjorie's' she continued. I knew I must do all I could to help. She wants me to keep Helen and John out of the way till after the funeral, I thought, and did wish that she had told me the truth.

Of course we had our usual warm welcome at "The Grove" and immediately felt at home. I did hope that Auntie Marjorie would tell us that Nana had died, so that I needn't go on pretending that she hadn't. But she didn't tell us, and I was faced with the biggest dilemma of my young life. If I asked how Nana was, Auntie Marjorie would be put in a difficult position, and would have to lie to me. If I didn't ask how Nana was, I would appear unfeeling and uncaring. I think we stayed at "The Grove" for about a week. I only asked about Nana once. 'I think she's getting on all right' was the vague reply. I didn't ask again. Each night I prayed that someone would tell me the truth the next day. Then I heard that the next morning Daddy would be coming down to take us home. At last, I thought, I can stop playing this awful pretending game. So Daddy had been delegated to break the news, I thought, and would probably do it on the way home. I was right. He was pushing John in the push-chair, and Helen and I were walking along beside him. We walked down Cowley Hill Lane and crossed into Gamble Avenue. Still no news. I was getting very agitated. Then, as we reached what was then the annex to Windlehurst School, and before we began to climb the hill, he said 'Nana has died, and Mummy is very sad, so we must do everything we can to cheer her up'. I was so relieved. A great weight had been lifted from my young shoulders. I said that I was sorry, but actually I was glad that we had at last been told the truth. Then Helen asked 'Will we be able to go and see Nana?' At seven years old she had not understood. 'Of course not,' I told her 'She's dead.' John said nothing. If Helen, at seven, was finding it difficult to understand, John, at four, probably had no idea what we were talking about.

As we turned into the drive, Mummy came out of the back door to meet us. No doubt she was genuinely pleased to see us again, and she was certainly making a good attempt to be cheerful. I wanted to say that I was sorry that Nana had died, but something told me that the subject was not to be mentioned. And it wasn't. It was forty years later, when Mummy knew that her own death was imminent that she decided to discuss the circumstances of Nana's death with me.

It was not necessary, however, for me to wait forty years before I discovered what had happened. We went back to school in September, 1943, and I was on my way home after the first day of the new term. I was standing at the corner of King Edward Road and Hard Lane with several

129

other Cowley girls, waiting to cross Hard Lane. We had been chatting, when Mavis, who lived next door to my friend Anne, turned to me and casually remarked 'Your Grandmother committed suicide, didn't she?' 'No, she didn't' I protested. 'Yes she did' I was told. 'She drowned herself in a water tub, and she had an iron tied round her neck.' Even as I denied that this could have happened, I realised that it probably had. It would explain all the secrecy surrounding her death. But the news had shaken me. Now I felt sorrier for Mummy than ever I had before. She had obviously done her best to protect me from the dreadful truth, so I must never, never let her know that I had been told. And I didn't. Not until she broached the subject herself, forty years later.

I think my Mother was relieved that, at last, she was able to talk to me about that terrible morning. Nana had got out of bed at seven o'clock and Mummy, after a disturbed night, had been dozing. But, after about ten minutes, she realised that Nana had not returned to the bedroom. Not able to find her upstairs, Mummy went down the stairs and discovered that the back door was open. She hurried outside, and turned the corner of the house to search the garden. Then she noticed Nana's legs sticking out of the full water butt which stood alongside the garage. She lifted Nana's head with difficulty, for the flex of the iron was wrapped around her neck. It was evident that Nana was dead, and Mummy ran out into Eaton Road and headed for Cust's house, which was next door but one to ours. Mr Cust was the Chief Constable for St Helens. He and a newspaper delivery man lifted the body from the water butt. By the time Helen, John and I were awake Nana's body had been taken away, a message had been sent to request compassionate leave for Daddy, and Auntie Marjorie had agreed to look after us three children for as long as was necessary. Mummy was too upset to go to the funeral, but she had to go and give evidence at the inquest. The coroner recorded a verdict of suicide while of unsound mind.

Often, during those forty years, Mummy must have looked at me and wondered 'Does she know?' And often, during those forty years, I wondered 'Does she know that I know?' One thing I didn't know, until we were finally honest with one another, was her reason for guarding her secret so closely through all those years. She had thought that, when any of us was applying for a job, we were certain to be asked whether there had ever been any mental illness in the family. If we admitted that there was, she feared, this would spoil our chances of getting work. She needn't have worried. I have never been asked this question, and I don't suppose Helen or John have been asked, either.

Auntie Aggie and
Uncle Frank

'Please hurry up, Helen,' we begged 'Or we'll miss the train.' Helen was dragging her feet, and, as protesting loudly at the weight of the two bags which she was carrying. We couldn't take them from her. Mummy was carrying the large blue suitcase in one hand, and was holding tightly onto John with the other. I was carrying the small black suitcase in one hand, and the brown paper carrier bag in the other. I had to be careful with the carrier bag, because, as well as the sandwiches and the biscuits and the comics, it had in it a thermos flask of tea. It was quite heavy, and the string handle was cutting into my palm. John was complaining, too, though all he had to carry was his gas mask. Would we ever reach the end of that long, dark tunnel at Earlestown Station?

It seemed a very long time since we had loaded the luggage under the stairs on the trolley bus at "the top of the Green." The first train had taken us from St Helens Junction Station to Earlestown. We would have to change again at Crewe. I hoped the platforms would be nearer to one another at Crewe. Before the war there were porters to help with the luggage, but now these had all been recruited into war work.

We were going to Birmingham to stay with Auntie Aggie and Uncle Frank. We had our emergency ration cards with us, and Mummy had baked a tin full of cakes. I think we spent nearly as long waiting on cold, draughty station platforms as we did sitting in the cold, dusty compartments of trains. We would amuse ourselves on the stations by reading the familiar wartime slogans displayed on the smoke-blackened posters. "Dig for Victory" and "Careless talk costs lives" were clear enough, but I was always puzzled by "Walls have ears!" As soon as we were seated in our compartment, we knew what John's first question would be - 'Is it time for the sandwiches yet?' After the sandwiches were eaten and the comics had been read we would sometimes play "I spy." If the compartment was not too crowded we would be able to relieve the monotony of staring at pre-war pictures of Rhyl and Llandudno, change sides and look at "Come to sunny Southport" instead. If the window was open to let in some fresh air, we would have to pull on the heavy leather strap to close it when the train went through a tunnel. Otherwise the choking smoke from the engine would come in and make us cough. It also showered us with black smuts. We were always filthy dirty after a train journey.

Auntie Aggie was Mummy's youngest half-sister. She was plump and she was jolly. We were sure of a very warm welcome at 622, Hagley Road West. By the time the train pulled into New Street Station we would be tired but very excited. We would struggle along with the luggage to the number 9 bus stop. Sometimes, now that we were at war, there would be a conductress instead of a conductor on the number 9. When we got to Quinton we would all look out for 622, for the buses stopped outside Auntie Aggie's house. Going into the centre of Birmingham we could wait for the bus right by Auntie Aggie's front garden wall. But on the outward journey, we had to cross over the busy dual carriageway to the house. Auntie Aggie would be looking out for us and would come across to help us with the luggage.

622 was a semi-detached house with a long, wide yard alongside and behind it. Here Uncle Frank had the warehouse for his wholesale confectionery business, the stable for his beloved horse, Dolly, and a lean-to shed for the Governess cart. Although he had a delivery van, I think Uncle Frank always preferred to travel by horse and cart. He had two notable characteristics. One was his deafness. 622 was quite a noisy house, because anyone wanting to talk to Uncle Frank had to shout very loudly. His large, clumsy hearing aid was never functioning properly. Uncle Frank's second characteristic was his obsession with thrift. We had always to keep an eye open for his latest economy measures. If he thought we had built up the fire too high he would lift off some of the coals and lay them on a shovel on the hearth. If he thought the gas was too high under the

pans of vegetables he would turn it so low that sometimes it popped out. And his habit of turning down the temperature of the oven did not improve Auntie Aggie's pastry! Dolly's droppings were carefully collected together and bagged for sale. There would be a bucket and a shovel in the corner of the Governess cart in case this was needed when out with Dolly. At the top of the yard the smell of chocolate would mingle with that of manure. A beautiful golden labrador retriever lived at 622, too. Rex would trot along beside Dolly, and would stretch full-length across the yard so as not to be left behind if anyone should happen to be going out.

Auntie Aggie's son John was nine months older than me. He was jolly, too, like his Mother. John worked very hard. He mucked out the stable, and was often sent down the road with the bucket and shovel to collect horse droppings. Sometimes he went out with his father to deliver the sweets and chocolates. Sometimes he went out with his father's good friend, Bill, to deliver the milk. Bill's sight was as defective as Uncle Frank's hearing, and eventually he went blind. Luckily his horse knew the milk round well by this time.

John's favourite hobby was constructing model aeroplanes and, if we could get one, we liked to take him a balsa wood aeroplane kit. When they were finished the planes were strung up from the ceiling in the square bay window of the front room. Then John would spend the next couple of days chewing the hardened bits of balsa cement from the ends of his fingers.

Edna was John's sister, but she was much older than John, and she was married. When we stayed at Auntie Aggie's we always went down the road to visit Edna and her husband, Norman. It was particularly exciting to go to Edna's house after her first baby was born. He was a beautiful baby with big, dark eyes. He was Christened Alastair James, and Mummy and Daddy were his Godparents. Sometimes I would be able to take him out for a walk in his pram.

While we were staying at Auntie Aggie's we would always go over to see Auntie Dorothy at 1056, Yardley Wood Road. This involved taking the number 9 bus into the Bull Ring, and then taking another bus out to Yardley Wood. It was quite a long journey. Auntie Dorothy was another of Mummy's half-sisters. She and her daughter, "Young" Dorothy, ran a disorganised, happy-go-lucky grocer's shop cum cafe. They were both very placid, and not at all business-like. When it was time for tea they would simply go into the shop and choose something from the shelf. If they needed to buy something from another shop, they would take a handful of money from the till.

Auntie Dorothy's kitchen smelled continually of chips, and her large, heavy, iron frying pan was black and thick with grease. But we had some good meals at Auntie Dorothy's house. At least, the food was good. The tea tasted revolting, because Auntie Dorothy sold only sterilised milk in her shop. Sometimes Auntie Connie and Auntie Ethel came to tea when we were there. They, too, were Mummy's half-sisters. The room behind the shop would get very crowded, and was noisy with lovely Birmingham accents as the sisters exchanged news. "Boy," the large, overweight, smelly dog with no tail, would retreat underneath the table.

Auntie Dorothy was very good-natured. Usually we waited till the shop was closed before we sat down to have tea, but if someone knocked at the door after it was locked, either Auntie Dorothy or "Young" Dorothy would go out to serve them. And even cook them some sausages and chips, if that was what they wanted. Cafes had a food allowance in addition to the wartime ration, but were not allowed to serve meals costing more than five shillings. I think Auntie Dorothy charged very much less than this.

One day Auntie Aggie's John took us on a trip across to Auntie Dorothy's in the Governess cart, just Helen, our John and me. He knew Birmingham like the back of his hand, and negotiated all the turns and crossings with confidence. I was filled with admiration. As we crossed the centre of Birmingham, we must have been a strange sight: old Dolly plodding along pulling the small Governess cart with four young children, being overtaken

Uncle Frank and Bill in the Governess Cart.

134

by buses, lorries, vans and even trams! We did have to pull up at the grass verge on one occasion, as young John declared that he could wait no longer to go to the lavatory. After he had relieved himself we discovered with horror that we would need to wipe his bottom! Fortunately I had a diary in my pocket, and a page torn out of that had to suffice. We were not at Yardley Wood for very long before it was time to set out on the long journey home. We just made it before dusk, and I expect Mummy and Auntie Aggie were quite relieved to see us safely back home.

Uncle Jim was the oldest of Mother's half-brothers, and sometimes we went to see him and Auntie Jennie when we were in Birmingham. They lived in Reservoir Road in the suburb of Olton. We were all very fond of Uncle Jim, who was kind and gentle, and very softly spoken. He was more like a father than a brother to Mummy, and had given her away at her wedding. He was very generous and always, when we were ready to leave, he would give us half a crown each. Auntie Jennie was a bit prim and very precise. Meals at Auntie Jennie's house were a bit like those at Grandma Menzies' house. We all had to mind our "p's" and "q's." Just the opposite from meals at Auntie Aggie's and Auntie Dorothy's houses!

A visit to 622 would not be complete without a long trip across Birmingham to Selly Park to see Auntie Polly. Auntie Polly was Nana's twin sister, and lived at 50, Cecil Road. After riding on two different buses, we finished the journey to Selly Park on a tram. Auntie Polly was small, like Nana, and always had some of her large family there to greet us. She would sit in her comfortable chair before the fire, nursing one of her young grandchildren, and we all had a cup of tea and a cosy chat. It seemed not to matter how many people crowded into Auntie Polly's small living room. The atmosphere was always warmly welcoming, and we knew that Auntie Polly loved us all. She reminded me of Nana when she spoke because their voices were the same.

Mummy was always happy when we were staying in Birmingham. She was happy, too, when her half-sisters came to stay at Cranley. I expect she wished that we all lived nearer to one another. Knowing that Mummy was so happy there, it was easy to relax at 622. Often we all slept together in the double bed in the front bedroom. I would wake to the familiar swish of the air brakes on the number 9 bus as it pulled up at the bus stop just outside the house. Then I would remember that we were staying at Auntie Aggie's, and all was well. It was sad when it was time to go home. Sometimes Auntie Aggie would sneak up to the warehouse and take a box of chocolates when Uncle Frank wasn't looking. Then she would hide it in our suitcase. Once when we arrived home and unpacked, we discovered that Uncle Frank had found our secret gift and removed it. Auntie Aggie was very annoyed when we told her!

On one occasion we three children stayed at Auntie Aggie's house by ourselves. I expect Mummy was enjoying one of her few breaks alone with Daddy when he had some leave. Auntie Aggie and Auntie Dorothy brought us home on the train. When we arrived, Mummy was horrified to discover that Helen and I had left our precious navy blue gabardine raincoats on the train! During the war there was neither money nor coupons to replace them, even if we could have found any replacements in the sparsely filled clothing stores. With trepidation Mummy telephoned the lost property office of L.M.S. Railways. The coats had been handed in. What a relief! As we went down to the station to collect them I vowed to take more care of my possessions in the future, and I suspect that Auntie Aggie and Auntie Dorothy were probably more thankful than anybody else to see those coats again!

Auntie Aggie and Uncle Frank in the garden at Cranley.

Two kinds of torture

The best way, I had decided, to face up to a visit to Dr Orton's surgery was to think ahead to what I would be doing after I got home. It didn't do to think too much about the actual dental treatment. It was an accepted fact that a visit to the dentist would be painful, and was a supreme test of one's bravery. I wasn't very brave. Drillings for fillings would inevitably continue until the drill touched a raw nerve, and a sudden and fierce pain would shoot through your jaw. There were no pain-killing injections for fillings, though you were allowed to have "gas" for an extraction. Very few grown-ups of my Mother's generation had many of their own teeth left, and most children had a large number of fillings. Nobody bothered much about restricting sugar in the diet, and extra sugar - for energy - was even added to baby's bottles! I don't think we cleaned our teeth very often, either. Mummy used to say that it was good to clean your teeth in the morning, as your mouth sometimes felt nasty when you woke up. It never occurred to us that we could have better avoided the nasty feeling by cleaning our teeth at bedtime.

Dr Orton was a qualified doctor as well as a qualified dentist. He had wanted to be a surgeon, but was prevented from practising surgery by his stammer. I think he had practised as both a doctor and a dentist in the army during the First World War. At the time he was practising dentistry Dr Orton was also studying Law. He was certainly a remarkable man.

Dr Orton's torture chamber was set out in the front room of a terraced house in Hall Street. The victim sat in a black leather chair, and was lifted to the right height in a series of jerks by means of a foot pedal. Then the round white porcelain tray on which were laid out the instruments of torture was swivelled round before the victim's face. Dr Orton planned his treatment carefully, and took his time over it. He was very proud of a large filling which had taken forty five minutes to build up around the small stump which was all that was left of one of my back teeth. On every subsequent visit he admired this filling, and complimented himself on his work. I still have that filling. It must have survived for over fifty years!

After the ordeal was over, Dr Orton would go to his glass fronted cabinet and find a sticky lollipop for his child victims, as some sort of compensation, I suppose. A strange offering from a dentist, you might think! It was one certainly designed to keep him in business. Not that Dr Orton could have profited a great deal financially from his dentistry. We never had a bill from him, and no-one else that we knew had ever had one, either.

The "middle" room at Dr Orton's served as a waiting room. Sometimes it was difficult to get in through the door in this room. It was not crowded with patients. It was crowded with old newspapers. Dr Orton obviously never threw a newspaper away, I think he had started to collect them during the First World War. You could tell which were the oldest bundles by their colour. Dr Orton's newspapers ranged in colour from pale grey to dark brown. Along one side of the room they were stacked nearly as high as the picture rail. From the picture rail on the other side hung several dusty prints of battle scenes from long ago. The picture above the small black fireplace was the worst. I tried to keep my eyes averted from it. Amongst the carnage of the battlefield were several badly injured horses lying dying in a pool of blood.

I tended to endure Dr Orton's torture with as few 'oo's' and 'ow's' as possible, taking the view that he was only being cruel in an attempt to be kind. Unlike Helen. Helen protested very loudly, and refused to sit still. Sometimes she even refused to sit in the chair. There was always a big scene when Helen had to go to Dr Orton's. Once, when both Helen and I needed extractions, it was decided that Helen might behave better at the School Clinic. So an appointment was made for us both, and we went down to town on the bus. I was to go in first. It was worth breathing in the horrible gas, for the treatment was over quickly and painlessly. A nurse helped me to wash out my mouth in the recovery room, then I went back into the waiting room. Helen was there, too. But she should have been in the surgery by then, having her teeth out. Once again, I was told, it had not been possible to get her into the chair. A scarf was wrapped round my mouth, and we went out to get on the bus. When it stopped at the Lingholme, Helen was put off and told to go back to school. I was taken back home to recover.

Mummy and I both tended to suffer from gingivitis, and our gums would bleed a lot. My gums swelled up as well. Dr Orton had an odd treatment for that condition. He used a metal rod with a tiny curled element at the end. When plugged into the electricity the element glowed like the filament in an electric light bulb. When applied to the gums this burned off the top layer of skin. Until the raw, red gums beneath had healed up I would need to be very careful what I had to eat. Anything slightly acidic would sting for ages! But my gums were then, according to Dr Orton, germ-free. Dr Orton explained his theories carefully, but took a long time to do so, because of his stammer. After several sessions of this peculiar kind of torture, I think he gave up. My gums continued to swell from time to time.

John was not generally known for making too much fuss. Except when he had his hair cut. But all little boys had to have short hair, and regular trips down to Bert Roberts' barber's shop in Duke Street were essential. As soon as he was lifted onto the high stool and swathed in the protective gown John would start to yell. We talked to him, we played with him, we distracted him in every way we could think of, but to no avail. He screamed loudly throughout the whole performance. This was quite embarrassing in a shop full of people. Bert Roberts was very gentle, and could not possibly have hurt him.

"Auntie" Nellie was not gentle. She was a friend of Mummy's, and had a lady's hairdressing business at her house in Moorfield Road. When Auntie Nellie did my hair, that was a torture nearly as painful as that to be endured from Dr Orton. The front room at 5, Moorfield Road was the waiting room, and sometimes I had to wait there for a long time. Auntie Nellie was a very slow hairdresser. The clock in the centre of the mantlepiece had a loud tick. If I was sitting there by myself and had no-one to talk to, I thought that that tick was enough to drive me mad. I couldn't even shut it out by putting my fingers in my ears.

Auntie Nellie's torture chamber was in her "middle" room. She, too, had a black leather chair like Dr Orton's. Here I sat while she did any necessary trimming, sending tickly snippets of hair down inside my collar.

On the day when I lost my plaits she snipped them off without even unplaiting them! After the trim, I would transfer to the upright chair before the wash basin, and lean forward. Auntie Nellie was only small, but she had perfected a strong scrubbing action on my scalp which brought tears to my eyes. And the rinsing water would run into my ears and down my neck. Earache for a couple of days was the inevitable price to pay for one of Auntie Nellie's hair-dos. It would take at least half an hour for Auntie Nellie to wind the wet hair tightly into the curlers. It felt as if she was winding my scalp into the curlers, too. Sometimes I think she was. I had the scars to prove it. Then there was the drier, which was invariably too hot. Auntie Nellie slid the curlers out without disturbing the curls. She never bothered to brush out the curls, and comb the hair into any kind of a style, so I would walk back home with a crown of little sausages!

If a "wash and set" at Auntie Nellie's was nearly as bad as a tooth-filling session at Dr Orton's, then a perm at Auntie Nellie's was even worse than a trip to the dentist. It took at least an hour to string up the curls to the electrical sockets which hung ominously from the huge circular perming machine. Then the machine would be switched on, and I gritted my teeth as it got hotter and hotter. The bits of scalp which had been wound in with the curlers would suffer horrific burns. For several days afterwards I would need to be careful to avoid the blisters when combing my hair. A perm took at least three hours. At least Dr Orton's torture didn't last quite so long!

Once I went to Auntie Nellie's for a perm straight from school. Auntie Nellie had promised to give me some tea. But she forgot. I arrived home starving sometime after seven o'clock, and Mummy was very annoyed. Auntie Nellie should have remembered to give me something to eat. She didn't even offer me a drink! After Nana died she and Uncle Leslie had come up to Cranley every Saturday evening and had enjoyed the substantial supper which Mummy always prepared for them. They genuinely thought that they were doing us a good turn by these Saturday evening visits, as they thought that Mummy would be lonely. I think she did enjoy having a chat with them, but she did wish they wouldn't stay so late. They were never ready to go home before midnight, and Mummy was tired long before then. And sometimes she would have liked to have done other things on Saturday nights. When Daddy was home on leave he would phone them and ask them not to come. Mummy didn't think he should do that. But she was glad when she and Daddy were free to go to the pictures together.

Mummy sometimes went to the pictures on Tuesday evenings with Auntie Jessie and Uncle Albert. "Auntie" Mabel came to babysit on Tuesdays. Auntie Mabel was Uncle Bob's aunt, and she worked in a draper's shop called "The Mart" in Church Street. I don't think she was a very efficient saleswoman. If we went to "The Mart" we always hoped that we would be served by someone else. Auntie Mabel could never find what it was that we wanted, and seemed determined to discourage her customers from buying anything at all. I think we led Auntie Mabel a bit of a dance on Tuesday evenings. We would tease her unmercifully. After bathing John she would come downstairs with her clothes soaking wet. John never misbehaved in the bath with anyone else. Sometimes for supper we would have bread and milk. If you broke the bread into quite large pieces it would absorb the hot milk well, and taste delicious. It was no use asking for bread and milk on Tuesdays. Auntie Mabel just could not understand why the bread and milk was not as good when she made it. She would say 'But I cut up the bread into very small pieces.' She insisted that I was just being awkward when I suggested that the bread should be broken, not cut!

Form 2b

Did we know, we were asked, what the difference was between French and Latin? I didn't. But someone else in Form 2b did. Latin was a "dead" language. It wasn't spoken any more. Everyone in Form 2a and Form 2b would need to learn Latin. We were those who, it was thought, might want to go to University when we left school, and no University would consider anyone whose School Certificate did not include Latin. Learning Latin grammar was quite interesting. It was a bit like mathematics, and there was a logical way to approach it. It was, I thought, much more straight forward than French, and I was prepared to enjoy this new challenge. As it wasn't a spoken language, I wouldn't have to be fussy about my accent, something which was a problem with French. But I was to find that there was one thing which made learning Latin a bit dreary, and that was the content of the passages which we were required to translate. The ones which weren't about Greek and Roman gods were about ancient battles which took place long ago in far-off places.

Always there were several new challenges when you went "up" a year at Cowley. Latin was one for Year 2, hockey was another. Now we would only play netball when the field was too wet to play hockey. We went to the storeroom off the pavilion, and were each handed an old and battered hockey stick. Proudly we marched down to the field to practise dribbling, passing, shooting and bullying off. Soon we would be initiated into the rules of the game, and I would be speeding up and down the field scoring goals for my team just like the girls in my Chalet School books. I was filled with a burning desire to be one of the best hockey players in 2b!

By the time we reached the Second Form it was thought that we were ready to be told "The Facts of Life." That is, if our parents agreed. Most of my Form had had their twelfth birthday by then, but I was still eleven. We were given letters to take home, in sealed envelopes, and asked to return the replies the next day. On the surface there was great secrecy, but we all knew what the letters were about. We had gathered under the tree on the "patch" at recess, and had discussed the likelihood of our parents giving their consent. I was unsure of Mummy's reaction. I thought that she would probably say 'No'. I still had it in my mind that such information was in some way "naughty." I handed over my envelope and thought that my suspicions were probably correct. Mummy seemed a bit more impatient than usual that evening, and was inclined to be short-tempered with me. It wasn't my fault. I hadn't asked to bring the wretched letter home.

The next morning I was standing in the kitchen and Mummy was plaiting my hair. I knew by the way she was pulling it extra tightly that she was either cross or embarrassed. I had begun to realise that both emotions generated similar symptoms. I couldn't see her face. 'I suppose' she said 'That you already know that babies don't come from under gooseberry bushes.' I swallowed hard and admitted that yes, I did. 'Do you want to hear about it at school?' she asked. I was astonished. The decision was to be mine! 'Yes, please,' I whispered, and, without another word, Mummy signed the consent form, put it in the envelope, and handed it to me. After we had returned our envelopes to school, we discussed our parents' reactions. Some of my Form-mates didn't even know whether their parents had said yes or no. I was proud to say that I knew that my Mother had said yes.

We were to go to Miss Hurt's room, six at a time, for the "Facts of Life" session. Each group would be there for twenty minutes. I think we were grouped by age, because I was in the very last group. As we waited outside Miss Hurt's door, older girls who passed by looked at us and tittered. They knew what we were waiting for, and we were embarrassed. At last we were admitted. Miss Hurt invited us to sit round a table. She sat opposite to me, with a small black book open in front of her. She proceeded to read passages from the book, and occasionally referred to tiny diagrams. It was all a bit difficult to follow, and I couldn't decipher the diagrams, as I was looking at them upside down. We didn't often get the opportunity to visit the Headmistress's room, and I began to look around. My mind wandered. I was day dreaming. The last time I had spoken to Miss Hurt it was to show her the commendation in my scripture exercise book, and that time I had only got as far as her open door. But now Miss Hurt seemed to be emphasising an important point, so I turned my attention to what she was saying, 'So you can't have a baby' she stated firmly 'Unless you are married.' After that she finished by making a brief reference to the physical symptoms which we could expect as we matured from girls to young women. 'But you don't need to worry about that at all,' she said. 'It's just a few days bleeding each month, and there are some very comfortable pads to wear. You'll be able to do almost anything except swimming.' So Miss Hurt had resolved one problem with which I had been wrestling. The reason adults could bathe was that the bleeding only continued for a few days each month: that was a relief! Then we were dismissed. That was it: the sum total of all the sex education on offer at Cowley Girls' School.

Those whose parents had denied them the opportunity of hearing Miss Hurt's little talk were then, of course, anxious to acquire their facts at second-hand. So we arranged another meeting under the tree on the "patch" to share our new knowledge. It was then that I realised, with horror, that I had daydreamed away the only opportunity I was ever likely to get of adding to my pathetically limited knowledge of "The Facts of Life." At seven I had worked out for myself that babies grew inside their Mother's bodies and now, at nearly twelve, I was still unaware of either how they got in there in the first place, or of how they got out. And my friends seemed as unclear as I was myself. I wonder if Miss Hurt realised how little we had gained from her brief lecture? The bit that Miss Hurt had said about marriage being essential to the process was puzzling, too. I knew what happened at weddings. When the couple knelt at the altar to be blessed, did a spiritual "something or other" descend from on high with permission for a baby to arrive? Besides, there seemed to be exceptions to the rule. Auntie Jessie's maid, Mary, had a daughter called Florence, but she didn't have a husband. I was pretty sure that she had never been married. How had that happened?

I wondered whether Mummy would ask me what Miss Hurt had said. She didn't. Despite our lack of communication on this embarrassing subject, Mummy and I had become much closer since Nana's death. I think she recognised that I was growing up. We did more things together, and sometimes she let me stay up later than Helen. Occasionally I went to the pictures with her. There were a lot of popular "tear-jerking" films being shown during the war, and we particularly enjoyed "Mrs Miniver." Although the newsreels showed brief flashes of bombed cities, war news was always presented from a positive angle. It was important to keep up morale. We were often treated to an extract from one of Mr Winston Churchill's inspiring speeches. And there was always a cartoon to make us laugh. At the end of the performance we all stood to attention to sing "God save the King." Anyone heading for the doors before the National Anthem had finished would get a disapproving look. The vast majority of the audience was fiercely patriotic.

Even better than going to the pictures was going to a concert at Cowley Boy's School. It wasn't the boys who gave the concerts. It was a group of musicians who hired the hall. Here I had my first introduction to the popular classics, and became familiar with the stirring tunes from Elgar's "Pomp and Circumstance," Holst's "Planets" suite and one of my favourites, "Finlandia" by Sibelius. Towards the end, the audience would be invited to join in singing patriotic songs such as "Land of Hope and Glory," "Rule, Britannia," "There'll always be an England" and "Jerusalem". I would forget that I couldn't sing in tune, and was supposed only to mouth the words silently, as I put my heart, soul and voice into the rousing words:

Cowley Boys' School in Hard Lane

145

'This Royal throne of Kings,
This sceptred island,
This earth of majesty,
This seat of Mars,
This fortress, built by nature
For her purpose......'

And we always rounded off our moving sing-song with all three verses of the National Anthem. We never questioned the words of the second verse at the time, though we would not want to sing them today!

'O Lord our God, arise,
Scatter our enemies
And make them fall.
Confound their politics,
Frustrate their knavish tricks,
On thee our hopes we fix,
God save us all'.

It was at one of the concerts at Cowley Boys' School that we learned that the Sadlers Wells orchestra was coming for a week of concerts, and that the musicians were looking for accommodation in the area. Mummy said that two of them could stay with us. When they arrived we discovered that one played the violin and one played the French horn. They were very nice, friendly gentlemen, and spent a long time practising their instruments. The French horn player was good fun, and he let me help to polish his huge instrument. The violinist was quiet. I think he found it difficult to practise, because his violin tended to be drowned by the noisy horn. When we went to one of their concerts, we were very proud of our own friendly musicians.

I don't know how much the musicians paid for their accommodation, but I think their short stay must have given Mummy an idea. Several people had suggested that, now that Nana's bedroom and sitting room were free, we might take in a lodger. Which was how Mr Cosgrove came to live with us. Mr Cosgrove taught English at Cowley Boys' School. He wasn't married, and he was looking for somewhere to live. He would be a useful lodger because English was still my weakest subject at school, and he might be willing to give me some coaching. Mr Cosgrove was very large. He was good-natured, but he had a loud voice, which I found rather intimidating. He smoked very smelly cigarettes, and even smellier cigars. When he had gone to school in the morning Mummy would open all the windows in the sitting room. When he had been to The Abbey for a drink at dinner-time on Sundays he would be too drunk to eat his dinner, and he would go to sleep instead.

When I went into the sitting room for my English coaching I was very nervous. It is difficult to write an English composition when you are nervous. My vocabulary was sadly limited, and Mr Cosgrove was doing his best to extend it. He decided that I should read the editorial in the Daily Mail each day, and then discuss it with him. I don't know how much Mr Cosgrove was paid for my English coaching, but I doubt that Mummy was ever fully recompensed for providing all his meals, doing all his washing and ironing, and cleaning his rooms.

On one particular occasion, cleaning his bedroom was a worse job than usual. Every Winter at Cranley, if there was a hard frost, all the bedroom wash basins would freeze up. Then the water couldn't run away down the plughole until the pipes thawed out. Mr Cosgrove didn't know about this when he arrived home from the pub late one night. Being either too drunk or too lazy to walk down the passage to the lavatory, he used the wash basin as a urinal. And it was frozen up.

Mr Cosgrove lived with us for quite a long time. When Daddy came home on leave they got on well together. At dinner-time on Sunday they both went to The Abbey. Mummy was not pleased when Daddy was very late for his dinner.

On one of Daddy's leaves he brought with him a guest who, in stature and in the volume of his voice, was rather like Mr Cosgrove. Major Bassett was very aimiable, and we all got on well together. The Major owned a large dog called "Gunner" who was, I think a pointer. Daddy was left in charge of Gunner when Major Bassett went abroad, so the next time Daddy came home, Gunner came, too. He was certainly a beautiful dog, but had a mind of his own, and was not easy to control. One day when Daddy was out Gunner decided to take a walk around St Helens. We were frantic with worry when we realised he had escaped. We set out to look for him, but he was nowhere to be seen. A large, lively dog can travel a long way in a very short time. We issued his description to the Police. How would we break the news to Daddy? What would we be able to say to Major Bassett? We were surprised when Daddy was quite calm. 'Don't worry' he said 'He'll come back!' We couldn't believe it. How could he locate his temporary lodgings when he had been here such a short time? But Daddy was right. Later in the evening, much to everyone's relief, Gunner returned. Poor Gunner did not last long after his visit to St Helens. Soon after he returned to his army home he was accused of worrying sheep. The only way that

Daddy could avoid paying a large sum in compensation to the farmer was to agree to have Gunner "put down" immediately, before he did any more damage.

After Mr Cosgrove left us we decided that we weren't going to have any more lodgers, and I moved into Nana's bedroom. The portrait of my Great Grandmother was taken down and put up in the attic. I had pleaded that I might suffer from nightmares if it remained on the wall above the wash basin.

I did my homework at Nana's little desk, which was now in her dressing room. I had a small electric fire there, too, and it was warm and cosy. Here, quite content with my own company, I whiled away many long evenings. When my homework was finished I would either read or amuse myself drawing plans for imaginary schools. They would all be girls' boarding schools, and have common rooms and dormitories as well as Form rooms, and I would have great fun planning the pupils' days and writing their timetables. Eventually Mummy would come upstairs and ask 'Do you know how late it is?'

Sometimes if I had a good book I would take it to bed with me, and I often had the light on to read long after I should have been asleep. Grandma Menzies lent me some of Auntie Eva's books. Today these books would be considered too nauseatingly moralistic. The "too good to be true" heros and heroines usually died young, and I enjoyed a good weep, finally tucking my sodden hanky under the pillow and dropping into a satisfied and comfortable sleep. There is nothing more satisfying and comforting than a story where the righteous get their just reward, even if this takes place in heaven. I thoroughly enjoyed "The Lamplighter," "Ever Heavenward," "Her Benny" and "The Wide,Wide World."

By now I was also thoroughly enjoying all the lessons at school. Even English wasn't too bad. Mr Cosgrove had helped me considerably with the techniques for writing a precis, and I was even beginning to understand the language in "A Midsummer Night's Dream". I enjoyed listening to poetry, as long as I didn't have to learn it by heart. I found learning poetry just as difficult as learning multiplication tables.

I didn't even mind staying for dinner now because, once the eating part was over, we had lots of fun. If the weather was fine we walked around the field or up and down the cinder track and chatted. As soon as the skipping season arrived we would skip with a long rope, each year adding more verses to the skipping rhyme "Nebucudnezzar the king of the Jews," and more intricate steps to the challenges which we set for ourselves.

And if it was wet we went into the pavilion. I always hoped that Miss Clarke and Miss Fuller were on duty. Then we would persuade them to organise our favourite marching game. Miss Fuller played the piano, and the tune that they played was the march from "Chu-chin-chow." We would be divided into two long lines. We marched down the sides of the room and met at the far end. Then we met in twos and marched down the middle. At the bottom we divided again, marched round, and came down the second time in fours, the third time in eights, and the fourth time in sixteens. The success of the enterprise depended upon teamwork. Everyone had to be aware of everyone else. It was when we were stretched across the room in lines of sixteen that the fun started. We joined hands, the lines joining up at alternate ends. Then Miss Clarke would take hold of the girl at the front, and lead the whole snake-like procession into intricate patterns. If one person had let go of the hand of her neighbour the whole thing would have disintegrated. That this never happened, though there must have been at least one hundred and fifty of us taking part, was a reflection of our enthusiasm for this fascinating game. I have never heard the march from "Chu-chin-chow" played since without being reminded of the pavilion at Cowley Girls' School.

I think it was probably when I was in 2b that we had the handwriting competition. I knew that if I tried hard, I stood a good chance of winning. Miss Neville Martin's tuition had paid off. I had already realised that a neatly written piece of work earned a higher grade than an untidy one, and several "commendations" for my work had inspired me to keep up my efforts to write neatly. It was easy to start a new exercise book with good intentions, but, to win the competition, I would need to continue to keep this up till the end of the Summer Term. I determined to try! All my exercise books were scrutinised at the end of the year. Three names were called out in Assembly, and mine was one of them. There was a problem, we were told, in choosing a winner from these three. So the three of us were instructed to hand in our "rough" books. This seemed to me to be quite unfair. If I had known that my rough notebook would be examined, too, I would have been much more careful with the writing in that. I didn't win!

Guides

How I envied the Brownies who were "flying" up to Guides! They were handed their "wings," and danced around the Brownie Ring before being taken through into the Guide horseshoe. Those of us who were not First Class Brownies waited until this elaborate ceremony was over. My darn was but one of several failures, so I was only a Second Class Brownie. Nevertheless, it was quite a thrilling experience to shake hands with all my fellow Brownies, and be taken by Pack Leader to be introduced to my Patrol Leader, who took me then to shake hands with Captain and Lieutenant and then with all my Patrol.

It was July, 1943. Although I had had my eleventh birthday the previous December, I had waited for my friend, Anne, to have hers in June, so that we could go to Guides together. As it happened, Anne was not in Guides for very long, as she left Cowley School soon afterwards to go to Huyton College. Her new school had been evacuated to Rydal in the Lake District, so she and I were to meet only during the school holidays after this.

Everyone in the White Heather Patrol was kind to me. I was very shy. Our Patrol Leader, with a white lanyard and a whistle, and two white stripes sewn to her breast pocket, was almost grown up and I was very much in awe of her. She gave me a tenderfoot card, which I took home and spent many hours studying before the following Friday. There were ten laws to learn, and a promise. There were knots to tie, hand and whistle signals to practise and three crosses to put together to make a Union Jack. I took it all very seriously. I had the whole of the Summer holiday in which to absorb all this new knowledge.

Mummy had the whole of the Summer holiday in which to find a Guide uniform. This was far more of a problem than passing the tenderfoot test. All our friends were requested to spread the word that we were seeking a Guide dress and hat. Auntie Jessie was looking for one for Anne, too. The dresses which were eventually found were very faded, except for the patches on the sleeves and the chests where all the badges had been removed. What a good thing that Mummy and Auntie Jessie enjoyed dressmaking! They unpicked all the seams, washed and ironed all the pieces, turned them to the wrong side, and remade the dresses. That my blue felt hat with the wide brim was rather on the pinkish side of blue did not worry me a bit. Fabric dyes in the thirties and forties did not stand up to sunlight as well as those of today!

As the night of my enrolment drew near I became more and more nervous. The ceremony was to be a very special occasion for our County Commissioner, Miss Christine Pilkington, would be our guest of honour and it was to her I would be making my Promise. I was too excited to eat much tea, and that which I did eat did not digest very well.

By the time I stood before this tall, imposing lady I was very hot, and my mouth was dry. I knew the words, but wasn't sure that I could speak them audibly. I heard my Patrol Leader introduce me and tell Miss Pilkington that I had passed the tenderfoot test. My tummy started to rumble loudly, very loudly. I focused my eyes on the shiny brown belt which encircled the waistline of the jacket of the navy blue costume worn by this very tall lady, and felt very, very small. I tried to speak loudly enough to drown out the rumbles caused by my ill-digested tea. Miss Pilkington had to bend very low to pin the coveted badge on my yellow tie. First I observed the stiff white blouse and navy tie, then the huge hat turned up at one side and decorated with a colourful cockade. I saluted proudly, and my small, shaking, sweaty left hand was grasped in a large, cool, calm one. Together my Patrol Leader and I "about turned" and marched back to our places in the horseshoe.

For many months I think I was a very quiet Guide. Although I loved every minute of the Friday night meetings, I was conscious of being a very small fish in a very large sea, and was constantly afraid of doing the wrong thing. The ritual aspects of the meetings appealed to me most. I enjoyed marching round into Patrol files for roll call and inspection, and then into a horseshoe for badge presentations and notices. It gave me the same feeling of security and satisfaction as those dinner-hour marches in the pavilion at Cowley with Miss Clarke and Miss Fuller. At 2nd Eccleston we had a strange tradition at the end of the meeting. After prayers we sang the Canadian vesper each week then we all turned with our backs to the centre, and looked outwards to sing "Taps." No-one ever explained this strange ritual. I wonder how it started?

For some reason the morse code appealed to me, too. I enjoyed swishing the flags round in their representation of dots and dashes. It is strange that, although I had found learning multiplication tables such a problem, learning the morse code presented no great difficulty. I learned it quickly and knew it well. So I joined the small group in the kitchen of the Church Hall ready to be tested for this clause in the Second Class test. Captain took the morse flags, and signalled some letters, words, and then a complete message. I wrote it all down in my notebook, but had been concentrating so hard that I hadn't noticed that most of the others had stopped writing because they couldn't keep up. So it was a surprise when Captain declared that we would have to abandon the test, do some more work, and try again another time. We went back to our Patrol corners. The other members of the White Heather Patrol could see that I was upset. Eventually I told them what had happened. My Patrol Leader said she would explain to Captain, and took her my notebook so that she could check my knowledge of the morse code. She was amazed. She hadn't realised that one quiet member of the group had succeeded when everyone else had failed. So I was allowed to go back to the kitchen and signal a message for her to read. As she initialled the relevant section of my Second Class card, my confidence grew in leaps and bounds! From that moment on I was much less shy and much less quiet.

I suppose I was a bit of a "swot" as far as Guides was concerned. We practised first aid up on the stage in the Hall. We applied large arm slings and bandaged sprained ankles. Captain produced a clinical thermometer. Our knowledge was being tested. 'Does anyone know' asked Captain 'What normal body temperature measures?' 'Ninety eight point four degrees farenheit' I said promptly, before anyone else had time to think. Everyone laughed. I was covered with confusion. I began to realise that being a "know-all" was not very Guidelike, and could be interpreted as "showing off." And, of course, I was showing off!

Shortly after I joined the Guides there was a huge Guiding Rally on the Rugby Football ground in Knowsley Road. We took our flag, and we paraded around proudly together with hundreds of other Guides. There was my friend Miss Christine Pilkington on the saluting base together with an imposing array of other important ladies similarly dressed with a colourful range of different cockades on the turned-up brims of their hats. What a great feeling it was to be a part of such a huge Organisation!

By now it was late Autumn and the evenings were very dark. No street lights were allowed. All the houses were blacked out. Car headlights were "hooded," and even traffic lights displayed only tiny crosses of colour. I had a torch which, in accordance with regulations, had a piece of black sticky tape covering half of its dim light. Walking home from Guides was a bit scary. I walked with Barbara Murray as far as her house in Moorfield Road, then I borrowed "Mac" for the rest of the journey. Mac was not a very attractive looking dog, but he had a pleasant nature. He was a black and white mongrel with a docked tail. It was fortunate that he was more white than black, because I could see him on even the darkest nights, as he happily accompanied me up Kiln Lane, along Rainford Road and up Kingsley Road. When we got to the top of Kingsley Road I would say 'Go home, Mac.' Mac chased off down Kingsley Road, and I ran round the corner and in through the Cranley gate.

One evening I arrived home from Guides carrying a brown paper parcel containing a large hank of grey, oiled "sea-boot" wool, and the pattern for knitting balaclava helmets. Another contribution to the war effort! I knitted several helmets during the next few months. I do hope they reached the airmen for whom they were intended, and were appreciated. They made my fingers very sore, for the wool was very rough. I wonder if the airmen's necks were sore, too?

As soon as the Springtime came I realised that there was one aspect of the Guide programme where I was definitely going to have problems. My knowledge of wildlife was woefully thin. A tree was a tree to me, and I had never noticed that some had differently shaped leaves from others, and that some had bark of different colours and textures. I didn't know a sparrow from a chaffinch and, apart from a buttercup, a daisy and a dandelion I had been content to label all the others "flowers." I don't think it had occurred to me that the sprig of white heather which decorated the emblem on my uniform was a picture of a plant which could actually be seen growing in the countryside. I had a lot to learn.

Despite this lack of basic knowledge where natural history was concerned, I enjoyed all the other interesting out-of-door activities to which Guiding introduced me. Firelighting was great fun! To pass the firelighting section of the second class test you had to light your fire using not more than two matches. We collected "punk" in little tins. Once our fire was alight we cooked "dampers." We shaped the gluey flour and water dough (with the dirty fingers with which we had just lighted the fire) into sausage shapes, and wound them round peeled sticks. As we held them over the smokey fire the already pale grey dough took on a darker shade of grey. Impatiently we removed our dampers from their sticks before they were properly cooked, stuffed them with jam, and declared that they were delicious.

Sometimes we went to Eccleston Mere to light fires. On the way we practised " Scouts Pace. " The distance from the Church Hall to the Mere was about a mile, and one of the second class tests was to cover a mile in twelve minutes at Scouts Pace. This meant running for twenty paces then walking for twenty paces alternately, thus ensuring that you did not arrive at your destination breathless. But you had to arrive at the end of the measured mile between ten and twelve minutes after leaving the starting point. It needed a lot of practice to get the timing right. And you were not allowed to take your watch with you! Twice I failed by taking only nine minutes, but I got it right in the end.

We played exciting games at the Mere, too. As "robbers" we crept around searching for "treasure" while avoiding being seen by the "cops" to whom we had to hand over our findings if we were caught with them in our possession. We never tired of games such as this, which remained a satisfying challenge even for fifteen-year-olds. Girls of the forties did not grow up as quickly as those of today! Sometimes our Patrol Leaders would go on ahead when we were going out, leaving secret tracking signs for us to follow. Stalking and tracking also formed part of the second class test in those days.

We stood in a horseshoe. Captain was clutching a pad of exciting looking forms. Those who wanted to go to camp this year must take one home. It was only to be a weekend, and we wouldn't be sleeping in tents, but it would be my first "camp." I could hardly get home quickly enough that night. My hand shook as I undid the button to get out the carefully folded form from my breast pocket. Mummy was doubtful. Never having wanted to do anything like this herself, she found it difficult to understand why I wanted to spend the weekend in an open field, even if I was going to sleep in a hut. But I was twelve and a half, and I was very enthusiastic. I managed to talk her round. We examined the kit list, and discovered that I would need three blankets, one to be sewn up into a bag. We chose the blue one to stitch up, the one with a "B" on it which Nana had given me when I moved from a cot to a bed at three years old. I would need an enamel mug, plate and dish, and a knife, fork and spoon, and we would have to sew a bag to put these in. We had an enamel dog bowl and an enamel pie plate. We went down to the market and bought an enamel mug. Together with a pillow case and our spare clothes, these belongings were to be rolled into a bundle and tied securely. Suitcases were not allowed. 'What will you do,' asked Mummy 'if it rains?' Ever optimistic, I was certainly not expecting rain. But it did rain! Tearfully I tried to dissuade Mummy from packing the large blue suitcase. She had been reluctant to let me go to camp in the first place, and was not prepared to consider letting me sleep in wet blankets. Either we took the suitcase, or I didn't go at all. Plastic bags were still more than a decade away, and the kitbags which would flood the "Army Surplus Stores" two years later were still, in 1944, being used by the army.

We met at the trolley bus terminus at the top of the Green. We wore full uniform complete with felt hats and gabardine raincoats. Our gas masks in their canvas cases were slung over our shoulders, and I was relieved to see that I was not the only one who was carrying a suitcase. It poured! In St Helens town centre we changed buses and got on one to Prescot. The conductor sympathised with us as he stowed our wet suitcases under the stairs and on the front seats. Eventually we arrived in the open countryside - Huyton!

We lugged our belongings up the long drive of "The Hazels." We were taken to a huge yard, surrounded by various outhouses. We were to sleep in a long, low building which I can only describe as a makeshift barracks. Probably it had been stables, then garages, and finally had been adapted for army use when what we knew as "The Big House" was requisitioned during the war for military purposes. The army must have left by 1944: we saw no sign of them. The dormitory was equipped with iron bedsteads and thin straw mattresses, and we were shown how to arrange our blankets on them. Then, each carrying a pillow case, we were shown a storeroom where we could fill it with straw.

Our two Guiders occupied a small room off the dormitory and took it in turns, throughout the night, to appear in their pyjamas to entreat us to be quiet and go to sleep. By the early hours of the morning they were desperate. They rightly surmised that the main problem was the sweets which were being passed around. Mothers anxious that their daughters should not be hungry had made sure that they had a bag of toffees to sustain them. Although I didn't like toffees, I joined in out of fear of being the odd one out. The tired pyjama clad figure in the doorway decided to check that the sweet munching was over. She asked each Guide in turn, 'Have you any sweets?' 'No, Captain' each replied. Either they had eaten them or they were lying. It was my turn. 'Yes, Captain' I confessed. There was still one under my pillow, I didn't want it and had not been brave enough to say so. 'I have one toffee' I added, much to her amazement. I think she was smiling. She didn't know what to say. Finally she said 'But you're not going to eat it, are you?' 'Oh no!' I had no intention of chewing any more that night. I had already had more than enough.

We emerged next morning, tired but still excited. The rain had stopped. The gabardine raincoats were still sodden. How did these inappropriately named garments acquire the label "raincoat?" All they did was to absorb the rain so that the inside was as wet as the outside. Out in the chilly morning air my nostrils were filled with that unbelievably appealing and soon to be familiar smell found nowhere else but in a camp kitchen: a mixture of woodsmoke and hot porridge. One of our Guiders stood beneath a canvas canopy stirring the contents of a large, black dixie over a blazing wood fire.

Before breakfast there was work to be done. My Patrol was to spread the bread with butter and jam. The four-pound loaves, the precious blocks of butter, and the pots of home-made jam were laid out on trestle tables beneath an open-sided wooden shelter, which was to be our dining room. A Guider sliced the bread, half inch thick slices and, mindful of the meagre butter ration, we spread them with butter and jam and arranged them on enamel trays.

Had porridge ever tasted so good? I doubted it. I vowed to put my porridge at home in the enamel dog bowl, to see if it was as delicious as camp porridge. Bacon followed. Someone had done wonders with the emergency ration cards. Then we finished every one of those wonderful jam "doorsteps." And finally, there was a painful lesson to be learned about drinking from enamel mugs. The enamel quickly absorbed the heat from the tea, and then you burned your mouth on the rim. When at last the tea was cool enough to drink there was another disappointment: it tasted of smoke!

A flagpole stood on the lawn in front of the Big House. We were well practised in forming a horseshoe, and we stood to attention to sing the National Anthem as the flag was broken. After the flag ceremony we discarded our hats and were taken on a tour of the grounds. When we arrived at the quarry we were given a list of things to find. I was glad this was a Patrol challenge and not an individual one, and hoped to learn some natural history in the process!

After dinner we were taken over to the Big House and were met by Miss Christine Pilkington together with her sister, Miss Constance. I hoped she wouldn't remember how my tummy had rumbled at my enrolment. We went inside. There were no carpets on the floors, and hardly any furniture in the rooms. Although Miss Christine and Miss Constance owned the house, I don't think they were living there at the time. We were taken up a bare wooden staircase, into a room full of grey army blankets: I had never seen so many blankets in my whole life! Our job was to take the blankets outside, shake them and fold them, then stack them neatly in a downstairs room. Another good turn, we were told, on behalf of the war effort.

Mummy was waiting at the top of the Green when I got off the bus, and helped to carry the blue suitcase up Kingsley Road. I had been away for only two nights, but had so much to tell her! A whole year to wait before the next camp, but there was no doubt that I was saying, with Eliza Jane in the familiar campfire song: "I'm going back to camp next year!"

Helping at home

'I'm taking you to school this morning' I said to John. He looked bewildered. 'But I've been to school' he protested, 'I went yesterday!' It was the second day of his first term at Windlehurst School. He was just five, and should have been going into the kindergarten at Cowley. We were all very sad that the 1944 Education Act had caused Cowley to be designated a Secondary Grammar School thus losing, together with its proudly unique semi-independent status, its well-loved preparatory department. Mummy had taken John to Windlehurst on his first morning, and had enrolled him in Miss Beezley's class.

The Cowley term had not yet started. This was John's second school day, and I was taking him. I tried to explain reassuringly that he would need to go to school every weekday, and hoped that he would soon enjoy school as much as I did. Windlehurst was very different from Cowley. The buildings were more modern, and had large, low windows. I soon found Miss Beezley, in a very large, airy room full of small tables and chairs. John eventually let go of my hand unwillingly. Fortunately he rarely cried. When I went to pick him up at dinner-time Miss Beezley called me over to her desk. 'What does the "L" stand for in the middle of his name?' she asked. 'He's John Laidlaw Menzies' I replied, and spelled out "Laidlaw" for her. 'I really think that now he is five, he should know what his middle name is!' she admonished. None of us had realised that he didn't know his full name, and taught it to him as soon as we got home.

It was not only the building which differed at Windlehurst. They used a different vocabulary, too. John was in a "class," not a "form," and he had a "teacher," not a "mistress." According to John, when Miss Beezley called the register, the response was "pleasant!" It was some time before I realised that he should have been saying "Present."

I was very protective towards John. If anyone appeared to criticise him I would jump to his defence. One day he stated quite firmly that he would no longer go to school in his lovely little Windsor-Woollie shorts with their elasicated waistband, and demanded "proper" trousers with braces, like the other boys. But the Windsor-Woollies had been bought new for school, and there was neither money nor coupons to replace them. Besides, we all thought he looked very nice in his new school outfit. However, when we discovered that our choice of shorts was "cissy", and that the other boys teased and pulled them down, the money and the coupons for a new pair of shorts and a pair of braces had to be found.

Soon John was able to walk home from school alone. Often, however, he had failed to appear by the time I got home from Cowley, and I would be sent out to look for him. Was it possible, I wondered, to travel such a short distance in such a long time? When we met I first tied his shoelaces, then undid the buttons on his coat, and re-buttoned them into the right buttonholes. Then I would kiss him, take his hand and lead him home.

When John did come straight home, he was rarely alone. Other Windlehust pupils discovered that the Cranley house and garden was an attractive play place and when we tried to send them home they would plead that there was no-one in at their house. Certainly no-one ever came to look for them. John was a hospitable host, and would invite them to stay for tea. Catherine frequently followed him home. She rarely spoke, and stood uncomprehendingly when we told her that it was time to go home. Eventually I would have to escort her down Kingsley Road. She lived at the small shop which then stood in Rainford Road near to the top of the Green. John always referred to her as 'my friend Cafrine,' though we wondered how you made a friend of someone who never spoke a word.

As I now went to Cowley on my bike, I would give John a lift to Windlehurst on my way. With my satchel and my gas mask in the basket on the handlebars, and John sitting on the saddle with his arms firmly gripping my waist, I would pedal round to Windlehurst standing up. It only took about five minutes. Which was just as well, for we were invariably late setting off. One morning it was very frosty, so I was pedalling more slowly than usual, and steering extra carefully. But when we got to the corner of King Edward Road and Princess Avenue there were some "setts." The surface being rough, I thought it would be less likely to be slippery, so I whizzed round the corner a bit faster. I was wrong. Setts proved to be more, not less slippery. John and I and the bike landed in a tangled heap at the side of the road. A passer-by helped us to our feet, and I was relieved to see that John had escaped without a scratch. He didn't even cry. I think he must have been suffering from shock. The grazes on my knees were not too painful. We walked the rest of the way to Windlehurst.

One day soon after this accident Mr Cust, the Chief Constable of St Helens, emerged from his gate in Eaton Road as I was pedalling past with John on my bike. I think he must have been looking out for us. He signalled to me to stop. 'You shouldn't ride like that, you know' he told me 'It's illegal.' For the next few days we walked to Windlehurst, and I pushed my bike till after I had taken John to school. However, as we were soon in danger of arriving late, we would revert to our speedier mode of transport once we were out of sight of Mr Cust's house.

After Irene left the only domestic help available was from those who were exempt from War Service. For a time we employed either elderly ladies or women with small children. We were indeed fortunate when Marie agreed to come and help us. Marie had been one of Nana's faithful maids in her younger days, and had worked at 22, Hard Lane before Mummy was married. Marie was kind and gentle, quiet and hardworking. She was spotlessly clean, had beautiful hair and attractive clothes. She was very well spoken, and did not seem to me to be at all like a domestic servant. But, although we were happy to treat Marie as one of the family, she had been trained to "know her place" and was, at times, embarrassingly deferential.

Mary was much more like one of the family. She had a young baby called Susan. Mary was unmarried, and she and Susan needed a home. So they moved into our small bedroom, with all their belongings, including Susan's utility cot. The only furniture available during the war was "utility." As its name suggests, this was strictly utilitarian, made with the minimum amount of material, completely lacking in any decoration, and usually without any paint or varnish. There wasn't much room in the little bedroom, but Mary and Susan lived there quite happily for several months. Susan was soon crawling around, and we enjoyed playing with her. She was a happy baby. She thrived on National Dried Milk. She would sit in her push-chair in the hall and watch Mary polishing the hall floor. Sometimes I took her for a walk. She was beginning to talk, and used some strange but attractive words. When the planes passed overhead she pointed her little finger towards the sky and shouted 'are-pee-pim!' Aeroplanes were often referred to as "arepeepim's" at our house after that.

If maids were difficult to come by, gardeners were even more of a problem. But we usually managed to find an elderly gentleman to help us with our huge garden. When Mr Owen left us, Mr Wright came. We children earned ld a bucketful for collecting weeds, and I helped only reluctantly, for this was never one of my favourite jobs. But I did enjoy helping with the cooking.

When we were making cakes, the margarine and the sugar had to be beaten till it was pure white before the dried egg mixture was added. I would be given a flat whisk for this task, and my arm would be aching before the colour of the mixture was finally approved. I soon learned how to make cakes and puddings. Often on Sundays we had Queen of puddings, one of my favourites. For this we would use two of our precious real eggs. The egg white was tipped onto a large, flat bread and butter plate, and I would again be given the flat whisk. There was an art to beating up the meringue. If you sat on the chair under the kitchen window, with the back door open, and sloped the plate very slightly towards the door, the cool air would be incorporated into the mixture. At least, that was the theory. In practice you needed a great deal of patience! I would be urged to continue beating until there was a mountain of stiff fluffy white mixture on the plate. As I worked away at the meringue my nostrils would be filled with the heady smell of roast meat escaping from the oven beside the kitchen fire.

There may have been a war on, but nothing less than a roast meat dinner with vegetables and a substantial pudding was acceptable for dinner on Sundays. Pre-war traditions died very, very slowly in our family. A cooked mid-day meal of some kind continued to be served every day, even when we resorted to wartime delicacies such as spam fritters. I don't think we ever had the famous "Woolton pie," because Mummy was just as capable as Lord Woolton of devising appetising dishes from our meagre food allocation. Her wartime rissoles were delicious. Lord Woolton was the Minister of Food, and frequently came on the wireless to explain how we could make the best use of our rations. There were "Food Flashes" on the cinema screen, too.

Why did Mummy's bilious attacks always occur on a Sunday? Sometimes we suspected that the supper which she shared with Auntie Nellie and Uncle Leslie on Saturday night, followed by a very late night may have triggered an attack. These days I think her complaint would be labelled "migraine." I knew exactly how she felt, because occasionally I suffered from the dreadful "sick headache" myself. Whenever you lifted your head from the pillow it would throb incessantly, and it was difficult to open your eyes because they hurt too much. Any movement at all would bring on dizziness and nausea, and the effort of actually being sick would cause your head to feel as if it was splitting into two pieces.

With an ashen face, and eyes barely open, Mummy would stagger slowly down the stairs and put the joint in the oven. Then she would go back to bed. Not even a bilious attack would stand in the way of our Sunday dinner. I would run up and down the stairs gathering instructions for the vegetables and the pudding, reporting back as each task was completed. Then Mummy would make a supreme effort, and manage to carve the joint and make the gravy. She went back to bed and we had dinner without her. By teatime she could sometimes manage a cup of weak tea and an arrowroot biscuit or a piece of dry toast. Auntie Aggie suffered from the same complaint. Her favourite "recovery" meal after she had stopped being sick was a plain boiled potato and a glass of milk!

Monday was washday, and we had the remains of the joint either cold, or minced, with potatoes and home-boiled beetroots with white sauce. If I was at home I would help to peg out the washing. This had to be done in the way in which Mummy had been taught at College. Hanging things upside down or inside out was not allowed. Fortunately I liked a tidy clothes line, so my efforts were usually approved. When the washing was brought in it had to be neatly folded, and anything which was too dry had to be damped down and rolled up tightly. I was taught how to iron the hankies. Sometimes it was difficult to see which was the right and which was the wrong side of a hanky, but Mummy always knew if I had got one the wrong way round, and I would need to unfold it and start again. We still went through the ritual of airing the hankies and, after ironing, they had to be put into the top of the kitchen range. Nana had always been very fussy about airing the hankies. After I became proficient at ironing the hankies, I graduated to pillow slips. Pillow slips were quite difficult, because of the starch in them. If you ironed in a crease by mistake, the only way to get it out was to wet the whole thing again and re-roll it.

School blouses were always starched, and before putting on a newly ironed clean blouse it was necessary to run a hand, with fingers outstretched, down the sleeve. This caused the two sides of the starched cotton, which would be firmly stuck together, to separate with a satisfying crackle.

Many of our clothes were not made from washable fabrics, and serge gym slips and gabardine raincoats would need to be "spot cleaned" with "thawpit" before being pressed beneath a damp cloth. During each school holiday we would tack down all the pleats on the gym slips before taking them to "Johnson's" for their termly dry cleaning.

Every week we made up all the beds with clean sheets. We turned the mattresses, straightened the underblankets, then put the top sheet to the bottom. Then we made up the beds with clean top sheets, clean bolster and pillow slips, then we replaced the blankets, eiderdowns and bedspreads. It took quite a long time. Oven cleaning was another skilled job. It taxed the memory. Having removed all the greasy iron components of the gas cooker, and dropped them into the hot soda solution in the galvanised bucket, you then had to remember where each piece fitted when the time came to re-assemble the hob bars and the grill. It was like a jigsaw puzzle. If you got one piece in the wrong place, then none of the others would fit. A wire brush helped to scrub the pieces clean, but also tended to stab the flesh on your hands, which were in rather a delicate state, the skin having been softened in the hot soda water. Everything was carefully dried on an old towel. To neglect this task was to invite ugly accumulations of orange rust to develop on the iron bars.

Cleaning the table silver was less arduous. We could sit round the kitchen table for this. It was a social activity. First the table would be protected with old newspapers. Then one of us would spread the "silvo" carefully on the forks, spoons, cruet and serviette rings. Only the knife blades were stainless. Another would be delegated the task of rubbing off all the polish with an old rag. Then a third person was needed to give the final shine to the silver with a soft duster. I liked the serviette rings. They all had initials on them, and most had been received as Christening presents. Mummy's and Daddy's matched, as they had been a wedding present. It was interesting that Mummy's was marked with a "B" for Becky rather than an "R" for Rebekah!

I enjoyed doing the shopping. Shopping during the war was relatively straightforward, but took a long time if you needed to queue for goods which were in short supply. There was no need to wonder what sort of bread to buy. There was only "the National loaf." This was slightly grey in colour and rather coarse in texture, but, we were told, had added vitamins and minerals to make up for any deficiencies in the rest of our diet. It cost $4^1/_2$d. One day I took the shopping list and the basket and a ten shilling note and set off across the waste land where Walton Road now stands. It was the first time that I had been entrusted with such a large amount of money, but Mummy had no change. By the time I reached Rainford Road the precious ten shilling note was missing. I was devastated! Tearfully I retraced my steps, searching every inch of the way. But I had to go home and confess the loss. Mummy was not, as I had expected, cross, she was just very upset. I think that was worse. She came with me, and we searched together, but we never found the lost money.

Sometimes I was sent out to collect money rather than to spend it. Mummy still collected for St Agnes Home, and I had a list of houses in Hard Lane, Kingsley Road and Rainford Road at which to call. I had to record the amount donated in the account book. I made a note of houses where there was no-one in, as I would need to go back there later. If I had the rent book with me, I would call at 22, Hard Lane, too. Our tenants paid 15/- a week. Always there would be a message about some deficiency in the house which would need to be rectified. Very often I would need to report the number of window sash cords which needed replacing. At the time I had no idea what a window sash was, but wondered how the cords came to be broken so frequently. When I got home I would be given 3d from the 15/-.

In addition to all her other household tasks, Mummy made all our clothes and her own. That is, when she could get hold of any material. Occasionally we had a parcel from America. One of Mummy's school friends was now living in America, and sometimes sent us a parcel of her own children's outgrown clothes. How we loved those American frocks! Once I had a blue and white frock with a sailor collar, and once I had one with flowers appliqued on the bodice.

Soon, we thought, we will be able to buy clothes like this in our country. We knew that the war was nearly over. Since "D Day" we had followed the progress of the army of liberation as it slowly crossed Europe, and celebrated each milestone as it was reached. In January, 1945, oranges arrived from Spain, and we were allowed 1lb for each ration book! Mistakenly I thought that everything we had been deprived of for five years would miraculously appear again the day after peace was declared. I also thought that all the troops would arrive home within a few days of the war ending. How wrong I was!

1945, and the end of the war in Europe

It was January, 1945, the weather was appalling, and we were going to Eastbourne for a holiday! Daddy had had his embarkation leave, and would be billeted in Eastbourne for a time before setting sail for Europe. Having served in the Royal Artillery for five years, it was discovered that the heavy tanks on which he had trained could not be taken on the narrow-gauge European railways, and he had now transferred to the Army Prison Service. In his new role he would follow the army of occupation to help to deal with the war criminals as they were captured.

We were all going to Eastbourne together on the train, and would spend as much time as possible with Daddy during our week's holiday. Time off school was no problem for such events. We had become as used to "Father's embarkation leave" as a legitimate excuse for school absence as was "Chicken pox" or "Measles."

It was a very long, very cold journey and, as usual, the sandwiches, the flasks of tea and the comics were very welcome. As I had no recollection of such things as restaurant cars on trains, or heated carriages, I did not miss them. Having installed us in the Angles Hotel at one end of the Promenade, Daddy had to walk to the other end to the Grand Hotel, which had been requisitioned by the army. Our hotel was anything but grand, but was one of few not to be "taken over." We handed over our emergency ration cards, and were grateful for the small portions of food which the hotel kitchen managed to produce.

It was windy, and bitterly cold. The sea was grey and stormy. The beach was cordoned off with barbed wire. The pavements were slippery with ice. And I was suffering badly from chilblains on my toes. It was cold in the bedroom. We had our hot water bottles, but I couldn't put my frozen feet anywhere near to mine because of the terrible itching which resulted from the effects of thawing out my inflamed toes. I slept, when I managed to sleep at all, with both feet hanging out from under the bedclothes.

Daddy had some time off each day, and he came to our hotel to see us. I limped around in my bedroom slippers. Sometimes we walked along the cold, bleak promenade to meet him, and putting my swollen feet into my walking shoes brought tears to my eyes. We found a chemist, who recommended "Radian B." It offered little relief.

Daddy always made friends easily, and soon aroused the sympathy of the proprietor of our hotel. In great secrecy, for he wasn't really allowed to sleep out, it was arranged for Daddy to stay at our hotel on the last night before we went home. Daddy had friends at the Grand Hotel who would cover for him at that end. I did hope our daring little plan would not be discovered. Fortunately all went well, and the next morning Daddy escorted us to the station, where we said our goodbyes.

It was nearly as cold on the train as it was on the promenade at Eastbourne. Nothing could ease the agony of my chilblains, and I suffered terribly on the way home. But nothing could suppress our mounting high spirits as 1945 progressed.

We knew that the war was drawing to a close, and we knew that we were winning. We had ceased to carry our gas masks around, and had become lax with the blackout regulations. Vera Lynn was singing "There'll be bluebirds over the white cliffs of Dover" more enthusiastically than ever. The news was mostly encouraging, although there were still war casualties. On February 9th we had some very bad news. I was shocked. Uncle Ernie's son Maurice was a rear gunner in the R.A.F. His plane had crashed near Brussels, and all the crew were killed. His body was recovered, and buried in a war cemetery in Belgium. We were very sad. Maurice was a fine young man of 22, and I had admired him greatly.

Although almost everyone I knew had suffered some tragedy during the war, we were all caught up in the excitement as V.E. Day approached. There was plenty of time to anticipate the great event. Street parties were planned weeks in advance, rations were saved and pooled, and feasts such as had not been seen for five years were prepared. We didn't live in a street. But we were going to a party. We were to join Auntie Marjorie's family in the garden at "The Grove". After the celebration feast there would be fireworks!

The shops were decorating their windows with red, white and blue bunting. Everyone had a small union jack at the ready, and we brought our big one down from the loft and dusted it. We bought some red, white and blue ribbon to tie in our hair. I had a length hidden in the pocket of my gym slip. I didn't want to be caught out if the announcement came when I was at school. Usually only navy blue ribbons were allowed, but we felt sure that the rule would be ignored when the end of the war in Europe was declared.

Would the great day never arrive? When it did, I think the thing which impressed me most was the ringing of the Church bells, which had been silent for five years. No-one minded when we tied the red, white and blue ribbons in our hair at school. There was a "thanksgiving" service in the Hall, after which very little work was done. Then we had two days holiday.

After all the celebrations were over, and the euphoria had died down somewhat, I began to realise that little had changed. The war was still going on in the Far East, food and fuel was still strictly rationed, clothing still required coupons, new furniture still had a "utility" label, there was no petrol for private cars, and there were still long queues for goods in short supply. We still ate the grey "national" loaf, coveted the precious tins of "spam" from the U.S.A., reconstituted dried egg powder and had almost forgotten what bananas looked like. But if anyone had told us then that food rationing would continue until 1954, we wouldn't have believed them!

Daddy was still in Germany, stationed at a small town called Celle, and it was to be many more long months before he was "demobbed". His experiences over the next six months were to warrant a front-page story in the St Helens Reporter. Celle was just fifteen kilometres from Belsen. A few days after the concentration camp at Belsen was liberated, Daddy was among the first British Officers to be allocated the horrific task of feeding and clothing the surviving inmates, restoring the power supply, and relieving the terrible conditions at the place. Joseph Kramer, known as "The Beast of Belsen" was in his custody for several weeks. When Kramer was captured, he was shut away in a refrigerator which was not working, for his own protection. But soon the troops managed to restore the electricity supply, and it was some time before it was realised that the refrigerator would be operating. By this time Kramer was stiff and almost frozen to death. But Daddy, sickened by the atrocities which were revealed at the camp, ordered him to be thawed out in order that he could be brought to trial for his crimes.

Daddy was responsible for showing some of the worst horrors of the camp to the leading citizens of Celle, including the Ober Burgomaster. He also witnessed Germans being guillotined at Wolfenbuttel for being in unlawful possession of firearms. Some time later we were to see a film of some of the least upsetting of the horrors of the German concentration camps at the cinema. We were sickened by the extent of man's inhumanity to man. But these were only pictures. Daddy had been there. Perhaps it wasn't surprising that he was a different person when he came home.

There were more celebrations in August, for V.J. Day. We were in Birmingham staying with Auntie Aggie on V.J. Day. These celebrations were not as thrilling as those we had participated in on V.E. Day. We knew about the devastation caused by the atomic bombs which had been dropped on Hiroshima and Nagasaki and, although this had finally ended the war with Japan, some of us were always to wonder whether the end really justified the means?

In the Autumn Daddy was finally demobbed. We were excited that he was coming home to stay this time, and not just "on leave." I had seen houses where returning servicemen were expected, and these were often decorated with red, white and blue flags and bunting, saved from the street parties in May. "Welcome Home" signs were strung across window frames. It seemed to me to be highly appropriate to recognise the importance of a returning soldier in this manner. So I tied our large, and by now rather tatty, union jack to the gatepost. Mummy thought it was a mistake. She warned me that Daddy might not appreciate the gesture. But I was confident that he would be pleased to be welcomed by the flag at the gate. I was wrong. My mother was a wise woman, and I should have listened to her.

Daddy had learned a lot of swear words while he was in the army, and had also acquired a very loud voice. When he arrived from the station and saw the flag he used both to good effect when he demanded that I remove the flag from the gatepost without delay. Having obeyed the order with shaking hands and a heavy heart, I disappeared to my bedroom in tears.

Later we laughed at Daddy's ill-fitting demob. suit and the ridiculous trilby hat, neither of which he ever wore. But some of my dreams remained for ever shattered. I had finally to accept that he had arrived home with mixed feelings, not all of which were happy ones. Army life had, in some ways, suited him. He enjoyed the companionship, the challenge, the excitement. In later years Mummy regretted that she had not urged him more strongly to remain with the forces in Germany. She would, she admitted, have been happy to have taken us to Germany to live as an army officer's family.

It was not to be. Daddy re-joined Uncle Sidney again in the radio and electrical wholesale business. And I became wary of the father who was sometimes difficult to recognise as the same warm, gentle, happy-go-lucky person I had known before the war. We were all to suffer during the period of his readjustment to civilian life. But I think John suffered the most. Understandably, I suppose, Daddy felt he had to compensate for the years when John had been surrounded by doting females. He was determined to "toughen up" his six-year-old son.

Although our recently returned father was, for a time, short-tempered with all of us, he seemed to look for any small excuse to chastise John. He would take him into the sitting room and close the door. I would try to escape out of hearing and put my fingers in my ears. I knew that John would be standing there tight-lipped and ashen-faced. He never cried. But I did. I think Mummy did, too. Once I heard her reminding Daddy that it was not appropriate to treat a six-year-old boy to the dressing down he might have given to a wayward rating in his regiment.

Poor John was about to have a big disappointment. We had built up in his imagination the taste of bananas as the most delicious flavour of any food he had ever tasted in his young life. We watched anxiously as he took a bite from his first banana. His face crumpled in disgust. He didn't like it.

John was now in his second year at Windlehurst School. Daddy did not like the idea of his son attending an elementary school and mixing with "rough" children. As an army officer his own "Public School" accent had become more pronounced, and a number of words and phrases which John had picked up at school were unacceptable to him. What a pity that John was not able to enjoy the advantages which Helen and I had had in the Prep. School at Cowley! Daddy was adamant. A new school must be found for John.

Christopher Else went to the "High School" in Ormskirk. This seemed to me to be a strange name for a small private school where prayers, lessons, dinners and physical exercises were all taken sitting in or standing by old desks crowded into small rooms. But at least the children attending the

High School spoke a language closer to that which we spoke at home. So John went on the bus into Ormskirk each day, and we met him at "the top of the Green" at teatime.

One day John came home from the High School looking rather embarrassed. Eventually he hesitantly extracted a beautifully knitted teacosy from his schoolbag. John was always good with his hands, but we had not realised that he was such a good knitter. It was a shame that he had to plead with us 'Don't tell Daddy!' He knew that either he, or his teacher, would have been in terrible trouble for introducing him to a feminine activity such as knitting!

During the Summer, crocodiles of High School pupils paraded down Ruff Lane to go for a walk in Ruff Wood. One very hot day I met the bus from Ormskirk, and was shocked when John got off. He was as red as on the day that he had been born, was sweating profusely, and his eyes were nearly closed. He fell into my arms and I don't know how I managed to get him up Kingsley Road. It was obvious that he was ill. The walk in Ruff Wood in the fierce sun had exhausted him.

Mummy was out. She would be at Auntie Jessie's house. I did what I could. I laid John on the chesterfield and gave him a drink. I covered him with a blanket. Then he was violently sick all over the chesterfield and all over the blanket. I got a bucket of water and attempted to clean up the mess. Then I realised that John was talking a lot of nonsense: he was "rambling". I was very frightened.

I hesitated before going to the telephone. Mummy would not be pleased to be brought home before she was ready. I explained that John had been sick and I thought she should come home. She was cross, and protested that she didn't leave us alone very often, and had thought I should be old enough to manage. But she came home.

When she arrived we put John to bed. Later that night Dr Merrick was sent for. John had sunstroke, and was very ill for several days. I hoped that Mummy would reassure me that I had been right to summon her home from Auntie Jessie's. But she didn't.

Form 3b and a real
Guide Camp

'We want the Ring scene, we want the Ring scene, we want the Ring scene . . . ' we chanted, our voices getting louder and more excitable with each repetition. 'We want the Court scene, we want the Court scene, we want the Court scene' chanted the opposition, trying to drown our refrain. 3b was undoubtably a difficult form to control. I am sorry for Miss Wood, whose job it was to resolve the argument.

Each form was to present one scene from the Shakespearian play which was currently being studied. It was the annual drama competition. Previously we had competed in Houses, now we were to compete in Forms. How sad we were when the House system was disbanded! We were never given a reason, just asked to remove the precious strips of coloured ribbon from our gym slips. My proudly worn orange ribbon had signified my loyalty and devotion to St Helena's House, and its removal caused more than a little heartache. We shared our indignation among ourselves. I don't think anyone thought of protesting to higher authority -in those days adults did know best! One thing is certain, if democracy had been in vogue at the time, we should have voted unanimously to keep our Houses.

We were, however, given the choice as to which scene from "The Merchant of Venice" would be our Form's entry in the competition. Form 3b was divided. As with many of my Formmates, my reason for siding with the "Ring scene" group was purely selfish. I was to take the part of Jessica, who appears in the Ring scene and not in the Court scene.

It was pointed out to us that the only fair way to resolve the dispute was by voting. Appreciating the logic in this solution, the chanting was quelled, and the pandemonium subsided. Those of us who, by this time, were standing on our chairs, stamping our feet and waving our arms about in a most unseemly manner agreed to sit down and take part in a secret ballot. Our cheer was very loud when the "Ring scene" supporters won by a very small majority.

Audrey Sanders took the part of Lorenzo. She was a good actress, and had always been better than me at English. I can still visualise her, sitting relaxed on the "bank", and hear her clear intonation as she recited:

'How sweet the moonlight sleeps upon this bank! Here will we sit, and let the sounds of music creep in our ears...'

I had heard this speech so often that I knew it well. My brief reply 'I am never merry when I hear sweet music' was a poor response. My voice could hardly be heard in the large hall. I finally admitted to myself that it would have been better if we had chosen the Court scene!

*Form 3b, with Miss Wood in 1945: Barbara is on front row, far left.
Beside her is her best friend June.*

To say that 3b was a lively form would be a gross understatement. I think "volatile" would be a better description. Most of us, at thirteen years of age, were blessed with a degree of self-confidence that verged on arrogance. We were undoubtably enthusiastic. We worked hard. We played hard. We were highly competitive, and self-opinionated to the point of rudeness. We must have been an exhausting Form to teach.

By this time I was often spending three hours at home in the evening doing homework. I was disappointed with any mark less than an A-. I was very selfish. I could not have been a very easy person to live with.

My chief recollections of Form 3b are of endless physical energy. We hit the ball in rounders almost into the gardens of the houses in Bishop Road. We hared up the field in hockey with single-minded fervour, we reached the ceiling by means of the ropes in the gym, and practised our vaults endlessly on the horse and the box in an effort to perfect them. We sweated profusely, and had reached the stage of puberty when our sweat took on an unpleasant smell. No-one had showers in those days, and we didn't even have any sports kit to change into. Our thick navy blue knickers with their elasticated legs and pockets for our handkerchief were never changed more than once a week, We had never heard of deodorants. In the gym we took off our gym slips and ties, and changed our shoes. That was all.

One day the gym mistress lined us all up along the wall bars and we sat down for a hygiene talk. It was brief. In future lessons we were to remove our vests and replace our blouses. And we were urged to use talcum powder under our arms to counteract the smell. I was shocked. I didn't think Mummy would approve. Talcum powder was only used for babies in our house. So I didn't even mention it at home.

Neither did I, at first, mention the fact that we had been offered ballroom dancing lessons, which were to take place during the dinner hour. It seemed like an activity of which my family would not approve. But I was wrong. When I casually mentioned the classes, shortly before the deadline for applying, Mummy was quite enthusiastic, and thought I should definitely have some lessons. I was thrilled. We almost filled North Block Hall. The taller girls took the part of the gentlemen, and we waltzed, quick-stepped and fox-trotted to the strains of Victor Sylvester's music on the old wind-up gramophone. When the mechanism slowed down, the couple nearest to the gramophone hurriedly rewound the handle. I loved the music, particularly the "slow, slow, quick, quick, slow" rhythm of the slow fox-trot. But the greatest fun was the the energetic polka, the military two-step and the valeta. Ballroom dancing became my latest and, at the time, my greatest enthusiasm. When Daddy came home on leave he bought one of Victor Sylvester's records, and we danced together on the wood block floor in the hall. He knew all the steps, enjoyed the rhythms as much as I did, was very light on his feet, and dancing with him was much better than dancing with the other girls at school.

At thirteen the most important person in your life is your best friend. And I had a new best friend. Her name was June Chalmers, and she lived at Haresfinch. During school recesses we walked around arm in arm and shared confidences. When it was cold we hid in the basement cloakroom underneath South Block and gossiped. When we had some grievance we gathered together a group of like-minded protesters and arranged to meet under the tree on the "patch" to share what we considered to be our righteous indignation.

On some Saturdays June would cycle over to my house for tea. On others I cycled over to hers. I liked going to June's house. Together with her mother and father, we played monopoly; long games which started as soon as I arrived, and sometimes continued after tea until it was time for me to go home. On dark Winter evenings June's father would check that my dynamo was functioning before I cycled home. The harder you pedalled the greater was the charge in the dynamo, and the brighter the front and rear lights. In some ways the dynamo was a very unsatisfactory device. If some road hazard caused you to slow down the lights dimmed, and if you stopped they went out altogether.

By this time June had been persuaded to join 2nd Eccleston Guides, and she often came home for tea with me on Fridays, then we cycled down Kiln Lane together for the meeting. By this time Barbara Murray had joined her cousins Anne and Margaret at Huyton College, so I didn't have her company on the way home. At Guides we were getting ready for a real camp this year, and would be sleeping in tents instead of a hut!

Each week we took along a small contribution towards the camp fee, and had this entered onto our cards. We took home the kit list and the health form. We wondered what a "camp overall" was, discovered it was a blue dress with short sleeves, and acquired one second-hand. We collected together the enamel plate, dish and mug, and wound a distinctive length of red cotton round a knife, fork and spoon. As instructed, we sewed up a small muslin bag, and threaded a drawstring through the top. We didn't discover till we arrived in camp that this would be filled with tealeaves, and dunked in the dixie of boiling water: the original teabag!

The health form mustn't be signed until the last minute, as it had to declare that we had not been in contact with any infectious disease for the previous three weeks. We held our breath on this one! There was a particular clause which caused Mummy some heartsearching: "May she swim?" She considered this carefully before suggesting 'I think I'll put "Yes, under supervision".' I was horrified. This would make me the laughing-stock of the whole Company! 'There has got to be supervision' I argued 'No-one will be allowed to swim unless a lifesaver is on duty!' Reluctantly, and to my great relief, Mummy finally gave in to my heartfelt plea on this issue.

Cowley Boys' School had a Sports Day on a Saturday afternoon towards the end of the Summer Term. How I wished that Cowley Girls' School could have had one, too. June and I went along, with many of our friends, to support the boys. There were large crowds, the sun shone, and we stood and admired all those athletic male bodies as they ran, jumped and manipulated their way through a series of obstacles. There was music playing, and a carnival atmosphere prevailed. The relief which had come with V.E. Day was still fresh and was, I think, affecting the tone of the cheering which greeted the winners of the races.

The "garden party" aura which pervaded events such as this was, I suppose, a relief from the pressures of school life, and I revelled in the relaxing of tension. There was an annual garden party which we attended each year at Eccleston Park. In the garden of one of the large houses there, we met to play and enjoy afternoon tea while our papier mache model houses into which we had slotted our donations throughout the year for Dr Barnado's Homes were opened, the contributions recorded, and receipts issued. With gay abandon we chased through the shrubbery, rolled down the grassy bank and played "leap frog" on the trim lawn. Life was good.

Life was indeed good. The weather was perfect that Summer, and the holidays had almost arrived. The war was over in Europe. I arrived home from school and leapt off my bike. I heard voices in the garden and chased down the path through the rose beds, jumping off the small wall onto the lawn. It looked like a garden party in my own garden! Mummy and Auntie Jessie were sitting in deck chairs chatting. Mummy had on my favourite pale green frock with the white pique collar. Anne and Margaret were there, too. They had already broken up for the holiday. We had tea in the garden. At that moment I knew that I was one of the luckiest people on this earth!

At school we had chosen our subjects for School Certificate. I had one too many. Nine was thought to be a sufficient number, and next term I was to "drop" Latin. Having determined that I was heading, not for University, but for the Froebel Educational Institute in London, Latin was no longer necessary. This would be a relief, as I was becoming increasingly bored by the Roman and Greek wars, although the structure of the language still fascinated me.

We finally said 'goodbye' to 3b and learned that, next term, we were moving to 4a. I was never quite sure of the significance of this change: probably it had something to do with the range of subjects which we had chosen. Now the holiday was here, and we were off to camp!

We had borrowed a kit bag and a haversack. We took the kit bag, as instructed, to the Congs. Church during the week before the camp. It was to go ahead of us in a railway luggage van. We handed over our emergency ration cards. We would meet at the station on Saturday with our packed lunch in our haversacks. There had been another disagreement with Mummy, when she argued that my pyjamas should be in my haversack, and not in my kit bag. 'Then' she argued 'if the luggage gets lost, at least you will be able to go to bed.' She really had no idea about camping! 'How can we go to bed' I pointed out 'If the tents and the blankets haven't arrived?' Mummy still didn't understand why I wanted to go to camp at all. She knew that she would never have wanted to partake in such strange, uncivilised activities.

We met at the station, and the slow local train stopped at Garswood and Bryn before finally pulling into Wigan Station. Here we waited on the draughty platform for the train to Blackburn. Our excitement kept us warm. On the Blackburn train we ate our sandwiches then, on Blackburn Station, had another wait for the train to Clitheroe. By the time we reached Clitheroe we felt we were in another world, though we were actually a mere 45 miles from home! We were directed to a stationary luggage van which, when unlocked, revealed all the camp equipment and our kit bags. The lorry was waiting, and we loaded it up, then climbed on ourselves, sitting on kit bags and tents, On the short trip to Waddow we sang at the tops of our voices. I had never ridden on the back of a lorry before: I think the experience gave us all a thrill.

Camping was hard work, but great fun. I tackled all the jobs with enthusiasm, and loved every minute of it. After pitching our tents on "Hill Top" site we took our palliasse covers and our pillow slips down to an outhouse to fill them with straw. The next morning, when we came to encase our bedding in the rubber groundsheets those of us who were inexperienced campers all realised that we had been far too generous with

176

the straw! On the first night, when I got into bed I was quite warm, and generously donated one of my spare blankets to the girl lying next to me, who was cold. I regretted this in the early hours of the morning.

The bucket lavatories, which we must remember to call "lats" were housed in little wooden huts. We kept turning round to look for the chain to pull, and there was none! I wondered whether the strong, unpleasant smell of the thick, tarry black elsan fluid was any improvement on the smell which would have resulted from using no fluid at all. I don't remember either washing or cleaning my teeth at this camp: it is quite likely that I didn't bother.

But I do remember the syrup of figs. It came in a very large bottle, and was dispensed from a teaspoon on the third evening after we were all in bed. No excuses were accepted, though many were offered. Everyone was dosed with the same spoon, which wasn't even wiped until it had circulated around every mouth in the camp.

When the weather was dry we enjoyed our meals sitting on groundsheets in horseshoe formation out in the field. When it was wet we crowded inside a bell tent where there was insufficient elbow room to wield a knife and fork satisfactorily, and where our soggy gabardine raincoats dripped onto our plates. We washed up in lukewarm water, and the grease floated on the water and congealed on the sides of the zinc bowls. Occasionally we were offered a lump of soda with which to attempt to disperse it. We collected wood for the fire, and learned to discard the "green" pieces and the "rotten" pieces. We broke our nails and got our camp overalls incredibly dirty. We lugged heavy zinc buckets full of water from the tap to the water bin, and the water slopped over the top and down inside our wellies. We peeled potatoes and carrots with blunt knives and wished we had brought a potato peeler from home. The only sharp knife was strictly for the use of the Guiders when they cut the bread. We spread loaf after loaf with butter and jam and, when the butter ran out, with jam. And I expect we also spread the bread with the grime which had gathered in our cracked fingers, from the wood, the potatoes and the wood-smoked dixies. Despite these apparent health hazards, we all remained strong and healthy.

During the afternoons we played rounders and we swam in the river. There was a special roped-off area for swimming. You had to demonstrate your ability to swim before you were allowed out of reach of the bank where Lieutenant stood clutching a long coil of rope, ready to rescue anyone in difficulties. The water was very cold and slightly murky. We squealed with delight as we swam among the weeds and with the tiny tiddlers.

In the evening we sat in a circle and learned lots of new songs as well as repeating those we knew well. We divided into rounds for "Kookaburra" and "White coral bells," we knelt with arms folded and declared that we were the "Red Men, tall and quaint, in our feathers and warpaint." We never tired of singing about Eliza Jane's camp disasters, such as the flag blowing away, and having dinner at half past two. This could never have happened in our camp! We made up extra verses to nonsense ditties which were already far too long. And finally we calmed down with memorable refrains such as "O how lovely is the evening." And it was. We stood around drinking strong, watery cocoa, and eating any leftovers from the day's meals. We went to bed tired but too excited to sleep, and whispered far into the night. We peeped under the canvas and could see Captain and Lieutenant silhouetted in the light from the embers of the fire, chatting and smoking the last cigarette of the day.

On Friday evening we joined with the campers from the other sites at Waddow at a huge campfire. We took along our "sitters" and joined in a huge circle around the towering fire. We all knew the same songs, and the feeling of belonging to such a large community of like-minded people was immensely satisfying. We made a loud, joyful noise which I was sure could be heard in Clitheroe. When we sang "The Tree Song" I thought it was the most beautiful sound I had ever heard. But the song which moved me the most was "The Peace of the River": 'When I learn to live serenely' we sang 'cares will cease.' What incredibly inspiring words! We stood and sang "Taps." We said 'goodnight,' and shone our torches through the darkness as we crossed the hill to our own site. It had been a truly magical end to a perfect week, and we were all sad that it was over.

After we had packed up the next day, we were asked to stand in a large circle. Captain stood in the centre holding a bucket. Then she started to throw out some small screws of paper which we ran forward to catch. Those of us who were lucky found a small portion of the remains of the week's food ration, which we could take home with us, My lucky catch contained about three teaspoonful of precious tea leaves. Some of my friends had about the same amount of sugar. We stowed the parcels away carefully in our haversacks. What better present to take home to our mothers!

Mummy met me at the station, and I am sure that I did not stop talking all the way home. Having unpacked my haversack and handed over the precious gift of tea, I unwrapped what remained of my packed lunch: the last of my delicious camp doorsteps. Mummy was horrified when she saw it, but I assured her that it tasted even better than the thin pieces of bread and butter which she usually served. Eventually I stopped talking long enough to get into the bath. I know that Mummy was upset when she saw the state of my hands. She wanted to know whether I had done all the chores for the whole camp for the whole week. I assured her that I had only done my share. She scrubbed my neck, but declared that only time could rectify the damage done to my finger nails. I was asleep as soon as my head touched the pillow, and slept until mid-afternoon the following day.

By the end of that holiday my long suffering family must have been utterly weary of listening to performances, with all the actions, of every campfire song I knew. Even poor Auntie Aggie had to suffer for, soon after the camp, we went down to Birmingham for a family holiday.

Form 4a and a
Masonic Ladies' Night

'With proud thanksgiving, a mother for her children,
England mourns for her dead across the sea.'

Laurence Binyon's poem had been written after the First World War,
but we were easily able to relate it to the war which we had just experienced.
This sad poem, "For the Fallen," was in the book which had been set for
our School Certificate study, "An Anthology of Modern Verse". Such
poems did not fail to move us emotionally. We empathised with Rupert
Brooke's soldier, who asked:

'If I should die, think only this of me:
That there's some corner of a foreign field
That is for ever England'.

We were all immensely patriotic, and loved, too, the sad wartime dramas
which were being shown at the cinema such as "Reach for the stars."

I enjoyed the words and the rhythm of poetry. Why was I so poor at
English in school? My essays were short, stilted and naive. They were
unadventurous and mundane. But when one of my comics (was it "Girls'
Crystal" or "School Friend?") announced a competition for a children's
story I entered with enthusiasm, and won! When my prize arrived it was a
book. All I can remember about this book is that the cover had been fixed
on upside down. It was rather disappointing.

180

In spite of my poor performance in English Literature I was enjoying reading "Macbeth." We had fun acting the part of the witches, and the story-line seemed easier to follow than that in "The Merchant of Venice." Professional actors were performing "Macbeth" in the hall at Childwall Valley High School, and it had been arranged for all of us to go over to Liverpool to see it. The bus journey was almost as exciting as the play! By that time we were familiar with the dialogue, and thoroughly enjoyed the stage performance. The final scene caused us a great deal of amusement, and was the main talking point on the way home. Just before Macduff comes onto the stage bearing Macbeth's head, Siward speaks the lines:

'Had I as many sons as I had hairs,
I would not wish them a fairer death.'

And the gentleman who was taking the part of Siward was completely bald! The irony was not lost on us.

How we wished that "Macbeth" was to be our School Certificate play. But next year the "set" play was "Hamlet", and we had been warned that this would be much more difficult.

In 4a we were much more serious about our work than we had been in 3b. Preparation for School Certificate had begun in earnest and, although the exam was almost two years away, we had begun to work through some of the questions on past papers. It was a bit scary. Barring last minute misfortunes I could guarantee an A in Maths. But what about English? A failure in English would mean no School Certificate at all, no matter how well I did in other subjects, The whole lot would have to be repeated! That would, indeed, be disastrous. I still spent many hours doing homework.

However, I always managed to break off to listen to my favourite radio programmes. Was it at this time that we laughed until we were breathless with Tommy Handley in ITMA? And held our breath in suspense as we caught up with the thrilling daily adventures of "Dick Barton, Special Agent"?

Life certainly wasn't all work and no play. Although we were thirteen and fourteen years old, in 4a we were still keen on skipping, and many old clothes lines found their way into school during the Spring Term. The steps we devised were as complex and confusing as the words of the rhymes which accompanied them. During the precious "recess" time we certainly had plenty of fresh air and exercise!

At home we were quite active, too. We went for long bicycle rides, toiling up Crank hill and Shaley Brow to Billinge, and exploring Billinge "lump." Often we took a picnic with us. Sometimes we returned via Washway Lane and Hard Lane, but many times enjoyed the perilous descent on the setts on Crank Hill. This route home could only be attempted if one's brakes were in sound working order.

We went for long bicycle rides.

John had a home-made wooden scooter for Christmas. I expect that Mr Foggett made it. We took turns to scoot around the many narrow paths in the garden. One day we heard an uncharacteristically loud yell from the back garden, and rushed out to find that John had encountered a stone which had tipped him over the handlebars of the scooter. One of his recently acquired new front teeth had snapped off diagonally, and Mummy was very upset. She took him down to Dr Orton, who painted the broken edge with some kind of preservative, and promised that he would be able to have the tooth "capped" when he was older. When Daddy got home he thought we were all making far too much fuss about a broken tooth. 'When he starts boxing he'll have far worse injuries than that,' he declared.

There is one other event concerning the scooter which is worth recording. After the war maids were still difficult to acquire. There was plenty of comparatively well-paid work from which girls could choose. So we applied to the Open Air School. Perhaps one of their "delicate" girls would be suitable for a not too strenuous job in a private house? They sent us

Catherine. She was fourteen, the same age as me, but she looked about ten. She was "childlike" in every respect, and her language and understanding was, I suppose, at about the level of a six-year-old.

Mummy made an effort to train Catherine. It was hard work, and we found ourselves looking after her in a similar way that we were looking after John. This wouldn't do: she was supposed to be helping us! She was unable to tell the time so, when Mummy was going out for the day, she made a sandwich and told Catherine to eat it when she was hungry. She would have no way of knowing when it was dinner-time! One day Mummy arrived back from shopping and, as she turned into Kingsley Road, she met Catherine who was scooting down the middle of the road at speed on John's scooter, her apron flapping in the breeze. Catherine left us soon after this episode.

It was shortly after my fourteenth birthday that I attended my first grown-up evening party. The occasion was the annual "Ladies' Night" at Daddy's Masonic Lodge in Liverpool. Uncle Ernie was Worshipful Master that year. Uncle Sidney was Senior Warden and Daddy was Junior Warden. All would have important roles to play in the proceedings. Mummy made me a bright red long-sleeved woollen frock, and embroidered the collar, the cuffs and the yoke. She bought me a pair of pure silk stockings. They were very expensive, and they were very uncomfortable.

Masonic Ladies' Nights are lengthy affairs. They start at about four thirty in the afternoon. I can't remember how we filled in the time until the dinner started, but I do know that I was urged to have a small glass of gin and orange. I lied when I said that I enjoyed it. The dinner itself took several hours. It was interrupted frequently by the sound of the knocking of wooden mallets on wooden blocks. Daddy was in charge of one of these mallets. It rested on the end of our table. After Uncle Sidney had knocked his wooden block, Daddy knocked his. Then there was silence for an announcement, followed by some ritual. First there would be a Latin grace, later a loyal toast and then the words 'Gentlemen, you may now smoke. ' (Some of the ladies smoked, too). After a number of lengthy speeches the wooden blocks were to be heard every few minutes with the announcement that 'Mr and Mrs X wish to take wine with Mr and Mrs Y.' Then the relevant parties would stand and raise their glasses to one another. When this ritual started, no-one seemed to want to be left out. Everyone wanted to take wine with everyone else. Eventually the coffee was served, then we ladies retired to the powder room to powder our noses. On returning to the meeting room we sat down to enjoy the evening's entertainment. This year the entertainer was a mind-reader. He startled us, and even upset some people, by knowing what we were thinking. He was blindfolded, and someone in the audience was chosen. I was extremely uncomfortable when they chose me. With his blindfold still in place, our "entertainer" described in detail the small brooch which was pinned to my frock. He knew my name, he knew what I was wearing, he knew how old I was. It was weird. We arrived home very late. I had learned a lot in one evening, and would know what to expect the next year when Uncle Sidney would be Worshipful Master, and Daddy would be Senior Warden.

There were Masonic Rooms in George Street in St Helens, and sometimes we went to dances there. Daddy and I danced together a great deal. I learned about "excuse-me" dances, "snowball" dances, "spot" dances, "Paul Jones" dances, and had a great time. We also went to dances at the Town Hall. Everyone seemed to want to show that, now that the war was over, pleasurable evenings of fun and dancing could legitimately resume. Although it was necessary for me sometimes to dance with other men, I always preferred to dance with Daddy. We used to show off. We knew each other's movements so well that we could dance together without even touching one another. By keeping my eye on the top button of his jacket, I could anticipate his movements and follow his lead faultlessly. We had fun demonstrating this skill.

None of our friends could dance as well as Daddy. I dreaded being asked to dance with Uncle Albert. He held me stiffly and very closely, and constantly trod on my toes. I have one misshapen toe-nail to this day which I have always blamed on him! Perhaps it is strange that all my recollections of dancing at this time indicate that I was partnered solely by gentlemen of my Parents' generation. I suppose that fourteen-year-old boys probably had little interest in ballroom dancing,

By this time I had forgiven Daddy for his reaction to my "welcome home" gesture, and our good relationship had been restored. He was interested in our education and, during 1946, there was talk about Helen and me going away to boarding school. Thankfully, it was accepted that it would not be a good thing for me to leave Cowley until my School Certificate course was completed. By then I should be ready for the 6th Form. Which school would want to take someone at that late stage? Mummy remembered that one of her friends had gone away to school late, and she had been accepted by Cheltenham Ladies' College. So we sent for the prospectus. It was very exciting. Scenes from all the school stories which I had read sprang into my mind, and I pictured the dorms, the midnight feasts, the revered prefects, the heroines on the hockey field, and the disputes between the rival gangs in the common room.

We went to Cheltenham, and Mummy and Daddy had a interview. They apparently passed the test, and we were to sit the entrance exam in the Spring of 1947. Among the information which we brought home was the news that Latin was compulsory. I would need to take it among my other School Certificate subjects, and Helen would need to learn some Latin quickly. At Cowley she was doing German as her second language in addition to French. So we both needed Latin coaching.

We found Mr Adshead, who taught Latin at Cowley Boys' School. He lived in Millbrook Lane, and Helen and I went to him for coaching for several months. I was almost as shy of Mr Adshead as I had been of Mr Cosgrove, not being used to male teachers. But there was really no justification for being afraid of Mr Adshead. A small gentleman, with his gingery hair and freckled complexion, he was basically kind and gentle. He couldn't have been more different from Mr Cosgrove. And he must have been a good teacher, for I soon found that I was getting very good marks for my work in Latin. Latin had now been substituted for Geography on my school timetable. I was happy to drop Geography, as I had never had much interest in far away places with strange sounding names. It was difficult for me to summon up any sympathy for those poor people in far off lands whose lives were so different from mine. I never understood the logic of the argument 'Some little African child would be glad of that' being used as an incentive to eating the rest of your dinner when you had really had quite sufficient.

Charities nearer to home had much greater relevance. 2nd Eccleston Guides had been collecting for Dr Barnado's Homes, and there was a Guide Company at their Home in Ainsdale. Three of us had volunteered to cycle over to Ainsdale to deliver our donation. We met at the top of the Green. I had the precious purse safely in my bicycle basket, and we had bottles of lemonade in case we got thirsty on the way. It was a long ride.

As we pedalled through Rainford we looked across to our left at the dual-carriageway by-pass which was under construction. It had been begun several years before, but all road works had been halted for the duration of the war, and throughout that period the short length which was tarmac'd was used as a tank park. Rows of tanks stood there for several years. When this road was completed it would shorten the journey to Southport considerably. Next we rode through Ormskirk, remembering to hold our noses as we passed the "smelly tower" in St Helens Road. This was the water tower, and we had not realised that the nasty smell came from the field of rotting cabbages beside the tower, and not from the tower itself. We noticed that an attempt had been made to erase the huge red crosses from the roofs of the buildings of Edge Hill Training College, which had recently been in use as a military hospital. Now the Students were to return from their wartime premises at Bingley. We paused in the town centre for a rest, and to admire the market stalls. I knew Ormskirk market quite well. We used to come out here on the bus when we needed knicker elastic. It was unobtainable anywhere else.

At Scarisbrick we turned off the Southport Road, and it was from here that I hoped my sense of direction would get us to Ainsdale along the country lanes. Some of the signposts which had been removed during the war to confuse any invading armies had been replaced, but not all of them.

Eventually we arrived at our destination and were greeted warmly by the Guides at Dr Barnado's, who had dressed in their uniforms in our honour. They were having a Guide meeting out in the garden of the Home where they lived. Two things struck me immediately about these girls: they all had similar hairstyles, and they all wore identical blue sandals. It was the first time I had seen sandals in any colour other than brown. We played games with our hostesses and sang songs, then they gave us tea before our long ride home.

At camp this year I was to be a Patrol Leader, in charge of a tent. With the voice of experience, I tried to explain to the uninitiated in the Patrol what to expect when we camped at Waddow again in the Summer holiday. This year we were to camp on Cragg Wood site. I have no doubt that I was a very bossy P.L.

We lined up outside the tent with our hats on for inspection. As Captain approached I saluted her, and accompanied her on her round of inspection. Our expertise with the gadget wood had not been great, but I did think it was unnecessary for her to rest her hand on the bedding rolls and the kit bags. The gadget holding them had been fairly secure till she did that. We had to start all over again. However, I still revelled in all the camp chores, though our turn as "Cook Patrol" was always the most enjoyable, even if it did mean that we had to get up half an hour before everyone else.

One day we were sent down to the river bank in Patrols, with a list of tasks to complete, among them lighting a fire to cook dampers and boil a syrup tin full of water. I realise now that it was intended that this activity should serve two purposes: it would offer an whole afternoon's pleasant occupation for us Guides, and it would offer a restful afternoon off for the Guiders. My Patrol would achieve neither. I urged them to hurry through the tasks as quickly as possible, then raced them back to the site at the double. I thought that we would be congratulated on being the first back home. But we were less than welcome to the poor Guiders who had barely had chance to relax on their groundsheets with their cigarettes and their cups of tea.

Some of the Guides in my tent were quite noisy at night. Captain came over, and I expected her to reprimand them for keeping us all awake. She didn't. She was cross with me for not keeping them under control. I took to heart this sobering lesson in the responsibilities of leadership.

It was while we were at camp that I was urged to complete the last clause on my second class test card. Could I name some wild flowers, some birds, some trees? I couldn't. Lieutenant would help me. She took me into the wood and named several of the different trees, thinking, I suppose, that I was noting the shapes of the different leaves, and the textures of the different barks. I wasn't. I was drawing a map of the wood in my

Barbara, right, kneeling as Patrol Leader, in charge of a tent. Left, kneeling, is her best friend, June Chalmers.

mind, and trying to remember the names she had given me when standing in different positions. It didn't work. When Captain took me into the wood later for the test I failed miserably.

When I arrived home I realised that the only option open to me was the permitted alternative: I could submit a nature notebook for the test. I acquired one or two nature textbooks, and discovered what, at that time of year, I should be looking out for. Then I took myself off for some nature walks. My favourite one was to turn off Rainford Road towards Crank, and then walk along Sandy Lane to Moss Bank. Here I actually saw a water rat in the stream. I cannot claim that I saw everything that was carefully drawn and described in my notebook, but at least it served to complete my second class test, and earn me the coveted badge.

Form 5a and Exam Time

Whose turn was it to decide which road we should take when we had turned left off Rainford Road into Stuart Road? I had been persuaded to take a brief respite from exam revision and to go out for a walk with the family. It was still a novelty, after the war years, to be going for a walk as a whole family. The warm feeling of "togetherness" was comforting. We often explored the rapidly developing housing estate between Rainford Road, Kiln Lane and Bleak Hill Road. When we walked with the Else family it was usually to Shaley Brow, or Billinge "lump" or Ashurst Beacon. Auntie Marjorie's family preferred the countryside. Mummy and Daddy were more interested in buildings than in hedgerows. Although many of the roads were still unmade, we would pick our way through the rubble, and eventually emerge into Coronation Road, where we could turn left and walk home up Kiln Lane.

Sometimes we went for a walk on Sunday afternoon. Pressure of work for School Certificate was a good excuse for a respite from piano practice, and I no longer went to "Weem" every week for a piano lesson. Now that Daddy was home he could take over the necessary visits to Grandma.

Although still only fourteen when I went into the fifth form, we in 5a felt that we were almost grown up. A few would be leaving school altogether at the end of the school year, although most would be going into the sixth form. By this time I had spent ten whole years of my short life at Cowley Girls' School, and the thought of leaving to go to Cheltenham Ladies' College made me appreciate how attached I had become to the place.

189

In the Spring term of 1947 would come the "mock" School Certificate exams, closely followed by the entrance exam for the Ladies' College. Some of my friends claimed to be smitten with fear and apprehension at the prospect of facing exam time. I was lucky. The anticipation of exams tended to have only a positive effect on my work, as the adrenalin flowed and provided me with extra energy to tackle what lay ahead. I plunged into the routine of revision with enthusiasm.

Daddy was studying, too. This year Uncle Sidney was Worshipful Master at the Lodge, and Daddy was Senior Warden. Next year he would be installed as Worshipful Master, and he had a lot of closely written small print in his secret little black book to commit to memory. This year I knew what to expect at the Ladies' Night, and enjoyed the long evening. I was glad that the entertainer was a singer and not a mind-reader. And there was dancing, too. Daddy and I both loved that.

Now that I had, at last, passed the second class test, I was eligible to earn some Guide proficiency badges. There was a local rule in St Helens that you could take two badges every six months. I chose gymnast and cook. We were tested for the gymnast badge in the school gym one afternoon after school. All the clauses were relatively easy, as we had covered them previously in gym lessons. But it was fun to have a special Guide gym session, and we were proud to have our certificates signed.

Those of us taking the cook's badge met outside the Gamble Institute in Victoria Square one Saturday morning. Upstairs we were shown into a vast kitchen with a row of cookers, which was used for cookery lessons. We had brought our aprons and our ingredients, and set about making our batches of scones. Then, each in turn, we answered questions on food values. These were not too difficult for girls who could not have avoided all the dietary advice offered to us on the wartime placards, wireless announcements and "food flashes" at the cinema. Lord Woolton had ensured that the whole population was aware of the values of vitamins and minerals, and how we could best maintain our health by using the food available to us.

It was a long wait before the precious badges arrived, and we proudly sewed them onto the sleeve of our uniform. Sadly, these were to be the first and the last proficiency badges which I was to gain. Both of our two Guiders were leaving us, and no replacements could be found. A kindly expectant Mother who had once been a Guider agreed to come and help us until her baby was born. She was too pregnant to fit into a uniform. A large, keen Company, 2nd Eccleston Guides were determined to continue. I knitted a pair of bootees for our kind helper's baby, and wondered what would happen next. For a time a rota of Mothers was organised, and they sat and provided us with an adult presence while we devised and ran our own programme. We Patrol Leaders took turns to make up games and activities, and I hope those who participated had as much fun as those of us who organised the programme. I doubt that much official testwork was achieved.

Unfortunately, it was one evening when we had no adult supervision when one of our number fell heavily and injured her wrist. We took her into the kitchen and ran the cold water tap on the rapidly swelling arm, to little effect. We applied a large arm sling from our first aid box, as we had practised so many times before, and sat the injured Guide in a chair at the side of the hall. And the brave soul insisted on staying until the end of the meeting, when two of us escorted her home to Brookside Avenue and explained about the accident. The next day, when I looked out for our injured friend at school I noticed that her broken arm was encased in a plaster cast.

As School Certificate time drew near I took less responsibility for organising Guide meetings, though we were delighted to hear that some of us would have the opportunity to join a Guide Camp in North Wales in the Summer holiday, run by Miss Gregson.

Armed with a set of "better than expected" results in the "mock" School Certificate, we set off with a certain amount of confidence mixed with apprehension to spend two days in Cheltenham. Miss Hurt was not pleased when we told her why we were going. She claimed to be disappointed that she was not to have me in her sixth form. The first day at the Ladies College was, for me, spent in a series of interviews, where my "mock" exam. results were discussed. It seems strange that, until that day, I had given little thought to the subjects which I would choose for the Higher School Certificate. Of course, Maths had to be included. Science, I thought, seemed to be associated with Maths, so I declared that I would study Chemistry, Physics, Pure and Applied Maths. With these subjects, I felt that my weakness in English might not prove to be too disadvantageous. With my "A" in Maths and a "credit" in Chemistry, I gave little thought to the fact that I had no idea what physics was about!

The second day at Cheltenham was exam day. We set off in the car from our hotel, and I was very excited. The usual pre-exam flow of adrenalin had my mind keyed up to tackle any challenges with which I might be faced. Daddy dropped us off at the archway and, over-anxious to get to the appointed exam room, I accidentally shut the car door on the little finger of my left hand. My mind, fully occupied with the main task ahead, had no room for pain. I opened the door to release the finger, shut it again, waved goodbye and hurried into College. Noticing that I was leaving a small trail of blood, I took out my hanky and bound it tightly around the injured finger.

There was, for me, only one exam, and it took the form of an intelligence test. Looking at the paper, I sighed with relief. These were just the sort of problems which I enjoyed! Armed with an array of information about those interesting families where one member was twice as old as another had been when the third was born, and so on, I merely applied Miss Willis's useful algebraic tricks to sort out everyone's age. What a relief to be tested on reasoning rather than general knowledge! When the exam was over we were treated to milk and delicious sugary buns with a blob of jam in the centre. Little did I know at the time that these buns were to replenish my energy during every morning break for three whole years from the following September.

When Mummy and Daddy picked us up we drove straight to the chemist to get some finger dressings. By this time the finger was beginning to throb. I was amazed to find, having removed the bloodstained hanky, that both the finger and the nail had turned a vicious shade of purple.

After any period of absence from school it was necessary, on the day of return, to go up onto the platform after morning prayers, and report back to Miss Hurt. She looked questioningly at my left arm, by now resting in a sling, and it took me quite a long time to tell her my story.

At last the letter of acceptance arrived, and Helen and I were both to go to Cheltenham in September, 1947. All that remained was to enjoy my last term at Cowley. And I did enjoy it!

Day after day we practised our vaults on the box in the gym. We were to give a gym display out on the field, and our families were invited to come and watch. We carried out the chairs for the spectators and the vaulting horse, the box, the forms and the mats. Revelling in the opportunity to show off, and bounding with excess physical energy, I glanced at the audience as I began my run-up to the box. Mistiming the vault completely, I flopped in an ungainly manner onto the mat. Embarrassed, I pulled myself together and thankfully got the timing right the second time around.

Then, at last, exam time was here again. This time there was no "mock" about it. This was the real School Certificate! French oral came first, and we found that our brief conversation in French was not too daunting. Miss Wood had prepared us well.We went home armed with the time-table for the written papers, and the news that we would only be required in school when we had an exam. The times in between were ours to use in any way we thought fit.

The desks were evenly spaced throughout North Block Hall, and in the gym. Notices on the doors reminded passers by to be quiet. The inkwells were clean and had been newly filled. There was a pristine sheet of pink blotting paper on each desk. The desks were numbered and silently, as we were allocated our places, we laid our rulers, pens, pencils and rubbers at the top of our desks. My fountain pen was filled from our bottle of "quink" at home, and I hoped it wouldn't run out. The pen would not write so evenly with school ink. The papers were distributed, and we awaited the magic words 'You may begin'. With plenty of practice in exam. routine, we knew the rules well. Planning, timing, and concentrating the mind had been developed to a fine art.

For the art exam we went up to the studio. For once Miss "Art" Duncan did not have to say 'Someone's inclined to talk.' In accordance with her instructions, she had erected a colourful display of objects on a table in the centre of the room, and the desks were arranged in a circle around it. All we had to do was to make an accurate copy. Little artistic imagination was required. All we needed was a keen eye and a steady hand. This was fortunate for me. It enabled me to achieve a "credit" in Art which I certainly could not have gained had anything more imaginative been asked of me.

Revising at home on the days, or half-days when I had no exams was a real treat. And, towards the end of exam. time, Mummy decided that she and I would have a day out together in Southport. What a thrill to be riding to Southport on the bus when everyone else was at school! We went to Broadbents for lunch and I was invited to choose anything I wanted from the menu. I chose grapefruit for a starter. This was a mistake, as I had forgotten that Dr Orton had just burnt off the top layer of skin from my gums. Why, I wonder, was he allowed to subject me to this cruel torture when I was in the middle of School Certificate exams?

Farewell to Cowley

We perched on our bikes and waited for the whistle. The aim in this race was to come last, not first. It was easier to ride slowly if you were standing on the pedals rather than sitting on the seat. Slowly, very slowly we progressed across the field and, yes, I did arrive last, and was rewarded with the number 1 ticket to take to the table where the results were being recorded. I was in the high jump, too. The custom at the time was to jump from a sideways direction, shooting your legs up before you and arching your back at the appropriate moment. Excitement was not conducive to calmly calculated timing, and I did not progress very far in the high jump. But I was confident of success in the skipping race. All those hours of practise which Anne and I had had in Eaton Road had ensured that I had become proficient with a skipping rope.

At last, Cowley Girls' School had an annual sports day, just like Cowley Boys'. Our enjoyment was enhanced in 1947 with the knowledge that all the important exams were now over. Homework had virtually ended, and we spent a lot of time playing rounders and practising our sports. In some ways I didn't want this Summer Term to come to an end. The thought that I would not be going back to Cowley was shattering. It was almost impossible to imagine life without Cowley.

Preparations were going ahead for the new term at the Ladies' College, and we were busily exploring all the avenues available for the purchase of extra clothing coupons for the uniform. Finally we had collected together a sufficient number of coupons, at great expense, and were to spend another two days in Cheltenham to visit Daniel Neal's, the official supplier. The list of garments required was lengthy, and "trying on" took all day. Helen swore that she would never wear the fawn lisle stockings, but we bought them for her, nevertheless. Shoes were my biggest problem. Daniel Neal's shoes were so narrow that, although I usually took a size 5, I had to have a 7 in order to accommodate my toes!

Two green, canvas covered trunks with wooden strengthening bands stood open on the floor in the sitting room. The initials "B.H.M." and "M.H.M." had been neatly stencilled on their lids in large black letters. June Chalmers and I were kneeling on the floor beside them, reading through the clothing list. We were intrigued by the items:

3 liberty bodices (Lower College)

3 brassieres and 3 suspender belts (Upper College)

June looked at my flat chest and pointed to the word "brassieres" 'That's one thing you won't need' she said. We both laughed.

The sewing on of name-tapes was a task which was allocated to anybody having a few minutes to spare. Although Miss Neville Martin's confidence in my sewing ability had been sadly misplaced, I was determined to do my share. The pile of white hankies was over-facing, and I started on the sheets and the towels. Socks and stockings were difficult, and vests and knickers were boring. Eventually there were more things inside the trunks than there were piled up beside them, and we were encouraged by the slow but steady progress which we were making.

The clothing list added a new word to our vocabulary. We would need 3 "mufti" dresses. We learned that "mufti" was a label for anything which was not uniform. How she managed it I do not know, but in addition to all the other requirements, Mummy had also managed to get sufficient cloth in the Menzies tartan to make us each a kilt. And, made to the traditional pattern, a kilt uses a great deal of fabric. I had a yellow polo-necked jumper to wear with my kilt, and it was my favourite outfit. We also each had our home-made grey pinafore dresses with handknitted jumpers. My third outfit was the red embroidered dress which Mummy had made for my first Ladies' Night. No-one could have started school better equipped, despite the desperate shortages following the war. I think the most problematic items were the two lacrosse sticks. Fortunately those were not needed till the Spring Term, and by then Wilfrid Mahood of Ormskirk had managed to acquire two second hand ones. Hockey sticks for the Autumn Term were more easily obtained.

Mummy knew that I should find it difficult to say goodbye to my Cowley friends, and suggested that we had a party for them. Nearly everyone in 5a came. We took up the carpet in the lounge, and polished the floor in there and in the hall for the dancing. We had quite a good collection of records of dance music by this time, and had added some Scottish dance music, too. "Strip the willow" and "The dashing White Sergeant" were current favourites. It never entered anyone's head that we might invite any boys. We girls were happy to dance with each other. We danced all the evening, with a break for the delicious buffet supper which Mummy had laid out in the dining room. We had a marvellous time, and I didn't want the evening to end. All too soon it was time to say 'goodbye.' I managed to hold back the tears until everyone had left. I assured them, 'We'll have another get-together next year.' But they probably knew as well as I did that this was unlikely to happen.

We did meet once more, however. On the appointed day at the end of August, we assembled at Cowley to learn the results of the School Certificate exam. The pleasure of my success was dampened somewhat by my attempt to comfort one tearful friend who had a failure in English. To fail in either English or Maths meant taking the whole lot again the following year. Without these two essentials you were denied any sort of School Certificate. Finally, bearing my results, I dashed round to "The Grove," which was close to the school, and used Auntie Marjorie's phone to convey my news to the family.

This year's Guide camp was on a farm in North Wales, and those of us from 2nd Eccleston were camping alongside those from other Companies. When we arrived we were pleased to see one familiar face. Margaret Edwards was a Sea Ranger now, and she was one of the helpers at the camp. When she was the Patrol Leader of the Primrose Patrol at 2nd Eccleston we used to call her "Muggins." I don't know what she had done to gain this nickname, but it may have been her cheerful willingness to undertake any task which came her way. And she was busy with one of these tasks when we arrived at camp. Having spent most of the previous afternoon, we were told, carefully arranging the store tent, a cow had come along during the night and demolished it. There was Muggins, calmly and patiently re-pitching the tent and re-organising the stores. We were very proud of her. I remember very little of this camp, except that on the last evening we had a fancy dress campfire. I think there were probably a lot of Red Indians, because we scavenged the farmyard for feathers!

For our family holiday in 1947 we were going back to Scarborough. Was it, I wonder, the enormous expense of the contents of those two green trunks which determined that we should stay this time, not at the "Wessex", but at a smaller hotel in a side street nearby? We visited all our old haunts. The North Shore swimming pool was a daily port of call, and we dashed to read the blackboard outside the gate on which the temperature of the water was chalked up. It was usually in the 60's. The nearer it was to 60, the more we shivered in anticipation of the impending shock to our warm bodies. The nearer it was to 70 the greater our smiling anticipation of an easier adjustment to the initial plunge. But we were never deterred completely by a low temperature. This was the year when John finally learned to swim, and I have a photo of my beaming young brother proudly standing on the edge of the pool celebrating his achievement. It was in this pool, too, where the last piece of damaged nail finally dropped off my little finger, and it and the finger stall were deposited in the rubbish bin.

John had just learned to swim in the
North Shore pool at Scarborough.

We used to laugh at the dinner menu, presented to us each evening although there was no choice of food. Each evening we gratefully received our small slice of nondescript meat with two vegetables and the dollop of gravy, followed by the spoonful of cold rice pudding topped with half a pear which was served in a small glass dish. For a long time afterwards, whenever we saw "pear condi" on a menu we remembered those two weeks in Scarborough when it was served to us every evening.

On the first day we toured the theatres to book for the shows. There were two variety theatres in addition to the Open Air theatre and the Floral Hall. The Floral Hall was a greenhouse-type structure about halfway down towards the beach from the South Shore. Here an orchestra played light classical music, and sometimes there was a singer. I loved these concerts. We enjoyed the variety shows, too. My favourite was always the "straight" man who supported the comedian. I wonder why? The Open Air theatre was in Peasholm Park. A lake separated the audience from the island where the dancers were illuminated with some very clever lighting. Here, for the first time, we watched synchronised swimming. It was most spectacular, and the show ended with a magnificent firework display.

The Else family were staying at Filey, and sometimes we went over to their beach to join them. We swam in the sea at Filey. Judith and Christopher had lilos, and we had great fun riding the waves. Sometimes they came to Scarborough to spend the day with us. It was a good holiday and, when I had recovered from the car sickness brought on by the journey home I realised how much I was looking forward to going to Cheltenham Ladies' College. Despite this, I wept on the day that the Cowley Girls went back to school. Eleven years was a long time to spend in one school, and I knew that leaving the Ladies' College, when the time came, would not be as painful as the wrench caused by my parting with Cowley.

The station wagon was waiting at the gate. The two trunks were well labelled. My labels proudly declared "St Hilda's House, Western Road, Cheltenham, Glos." and on the reverse side were the letters "P.L.A." (passengers' luggage in advance.) After the trunks had left, it was time to go down to "Weem" to say 'goodbye' to Grandma, and then to call on some of the neighbours to say 'goodbye' to them. I put on my Ladies' College uniform, and walked along Eaton Road to show it to Dadda Toddy. Now the overnight cases were packed with the last minute items. As this was our first term we would be travelling by car, and all the family would be there to see us safely installed in our new Houses. After this we were to travel by train. The atmosphere in the car was strained. For the first half of the journey we were obliged to listen to Helen's louder and more insistent protests about the discomfort she was suffering due to having to wear a suspender belt and a pair of stockings. Then she removed them. For the second half of the journey we worried about how we would explain her arrival without these required garments.

Helen's troubles were forgotten when I arrived at St Hilda's House and was shown to my cubicle in the dormitory. I was determined to enjoy this new life. Even at that time, though, I believe that I appreciated that I had had a remarkably privileged childhood.

I was now fifteen and a half. What a lucky girl I had been! Could anyone have had a happier home or a more loving family? Could anyone have had a better start to their education than that which was offered at Cowley Girls' School? What a wonderful collection of friends and neighbours surrounded us in St Helens! I had enjoyed holidays with the family and camps with the Guides. And there was surely a positive side to the war years, which provided so many opportunities for us to support one another, to show compassion, to develop patriotism and a sense of responsibility, to manage without so many things which today would be seen as essentials, and to appreciate all those things which we still had. No child today has the opportunity, as we had, to value a single piece of drawing paper or a Christmas annual, an orange or a banana. For these opportunities I will always be grateful. The 1930's and the 1940's were good years in which to grow up, and St Helens was a good place in which to live.